Social Currency

PAYING ATTENTION TO
WHAT EVERYONE IS
PAYING ATTENTION TO

REBEKAH BUEGE

NEW YORK

LONDON • NASHVILLE • MELBOURNE • VANCOUVER

Social Currency

PAYING ATTENTION TO WHAT EVERYONE IS PAYING ATTENTION TO

Published in New York, New York, by Morgan James Publishing. Morgan James is a trademark of Morgan James, LLC. www.MorganJamesPublishing.com

Proudly distributed by Ingram Publisher Services.

A **FREE** ebook edition is available for you
or a friend with the purchase of this print book.

CLEARLY SIGN YOUR NAME ABOVE

Instructions to claim your free ebook edition:
1. Visit MorganJamesBOGO.com
2. Sign your name CLEARLY in the space above
3. Complete the form and submit a photo
   of this entire page
4. You or your friend can download the ebook
   to your preferred device

ISBN 9781636981123 ebook
ISBN 9781636981116 paperback
Library of Congress Control Number:
2022950670

Cover Design by:
Rebecca Pollock

Interior Design by:
Irena Kalcheva

Morgan James is a proud partner of Habitat for Humanity Peninsula
and Greater Williamsburg. Partners in building since 2006.

Get involved today! Visit: www.morgan-james-publishing.com/giving-back

Social Currency is dedicated
to the version of myself
who looked for her worth
in the eyes of others.

You find
another way to live.
It's better here.

Contents

Introduction

What people do tells you a lot about who they are. But paying attention to what they pay attention to tells you even more. When something grabs your attention, it's because you see part of yourself inside it. It could be a part you're proud of, or a part you feel you're lacking. Regardless, you only pay attention to things that relate to you, in one way or another.

A few years ago, I realized the things I paid attention to stressed me out. I was constantly worried about how people saw me, controlling the opinion they had of me, and doing everything I could to impress everyone I met. But inside? I was exhausted. I was unfulfilled. I was impressing people I didn't even like at the expense of my own enjoyment.

It wasn't a new feeling. In fact, it had been my default mode for years, going as far back as middle and high school. Do you remember laughing and having fun at parties as a teenager, grabbing handfuls of Chex Mix from the parent-prepared snack table, and popping slices of greasy pepperoni pizza into your mouth? Well, I don't—because I never did. At one particularly memorable Halloween party during my junior year, I remember feeling my stomach growl beneath my 1970s go-go dancer outfit (the sexiest costume my conservative parents would let me wear out of the house). But there was a guy I liked at the party, and I couldn't bear the thought of him seeing me with my mouth full, so I picked up a napkin instead of a paper plate to make it look like I was eating less food. Then I put a few little pieces of Chex Mix on the napkin and tried to eat them as daintily as possible.

Fast-forward a few years to college, and in public I still only ate the foods that made me look the healthiest. I also drank whatever everyone else was drinking even if I hated it, which—in rural Minnesota—was mostly beer. So I drank the beer and ate the celery (a combination I don't recommend) and felt surprised when I looked around at the life I was living and felt disconnected.

I wanted to understand why I felt disconnected from a life most people were jealous of. Even though I hadn't reached nearly the top of the "mountain" I was climbing, I realized that each step didn't actually bring the fulfillment promised in movies. It didn't add up.

Given my background in economics, political science, and philosophy, I crafted a financial analogy to help wrap my head around what was going on in my mind. I needed to measure where my time was going, but more than that I knew I needed to figure out why my time was going there. Understanding a problem starts with knowing *what's* happening. Solving a problem starts with knowing *why* it's happening.

I realized it was deeper than just wanting people to like me. Everyone wants to be liked. This was different. I needed my philosophy training to get to the bottom of this one. There was a competitive nature to this desire; I wanted to be liked *the most*. At the root of this desire was a fundamental belief that my identity and worth was relative to other people and decided by other people. The attention I got from being an attractive woman conditioned me to expect and rely on that attention in order to feel good. Any threat to that attention—any competition for it—was met with jealousy and hostility.

This really bummed me out. It felt gross to realize that I saw myself and other women this way. But I figured this must happen to men, too. Surely, this is a human condition, not influenced by gender. I was right.

It turns out there are other measures we can use to decide the value of a person. I was conditioned to value myself based on my beauty and attractiveness. Others measure based on status and institutional validation. While others measure based on the power they have through tools like money or physical strength.

The further I observed and thought about how people value each other, the more I was reminded of my college economics classes and how currency functions within society.

But unlike the dollar, this form of currency isn't accepted by financial institutions. What you trade with this currency is social acceptance or social rejection.

In other words, it's a social currency. Depending on how much of it you have, you can afford different things depending on where you are, who you're with, and what those people value. But what's most interesting (and frustrating) about social currency is that, unlike financial currency, it's not valued the same in every transaction.

Every individual has their own conversion table for social currency based on what they personally value. I can walk up to someone and have them give me all their attention because of the way I look, while someone else across the room doesn't even notice me. Why? Because they're paying attention to different currencies. They see different things.

Which is why basing my personal value solely in social currency led to my disconnect, burnout, and general exhaustion.

But not all hope is lost. I'm not suggesting we do away with social currency altogether. It's a tool, and like any tool, it can be used for good things or bad things. What matters is knowing the difference—and choosing wisely.

Becoming aware of social currency helps you use it well. It helps you read people more easily when you meet them. It shows you what they value and what they might value about you, if you show them the right thing. Think of it like currency in a wallet. You have euros, dollars, pesos, and Ethereum. You don't know what other people have, or if they accept any of the currency you're carrying.

When you see euros in someone else's wallet, you're going to buy from them using euros. Someone else might be using pounds. Others are trading digitally in Ethereum or Bitcoin. When you go to transact, it's best to use the currency they value. This is not always clear, but when you learn about each currency and how people use it, your chances of picking the right one increases.

As I mentioned earlier, people also pay attention to things they lack and truly desire. So it may also be the lack of that currency that shows what you should give to them. Someone who greatly values Bitcoin and has nothing but pesos isn't going to be impressed by my pesos. But if I show I have Bitcoin, now I have their attention.

It's the same with social currency. This is how, as an introvert, I can get excited about meeting new people. Instead of worrying what to say or if the conversation will get awkward, I turn into a detective figuring out and analyzing what social currency this person has, what they want, and what they're faking. It becomes somewhat of a game to me.

Once I have my theory, I make a transaction. I place a bid for their attention by showing something I think they'll bite on. And it works.

This is how I quickly earn trust with private people, how I have subtle influence over everyone from executives at Apple to the people at the DMV, and how I walk away from every interaction not caring if they were impressed by me but focused on how I made *them* feel.

By the end of this book, it's my goal to help you separate your self-worth from your social currency. I'll do this by showing you what social currency is, why we're automatically wired to care about it, and how you can expand your social impact by understanding this mechanism that's been influencing human relationships since day one.

PART ONE:

Budgeting Attention

CHAPTER 1

What's in Your (Social) Wallet?

A few years ago, I was a young college grad with big corporate dreams. I had a strong desire to prove myself. I was well on my way to breaking out of the small-town pattern of an average job, average marriage, and average level of happiness. I wanted more and was willing to work as hard as I needed to in order to get it.

Sounds like the beginning of an epic novel, right? The triumphant journey of one woman's rise to the top? That's what I thought, too—which is why I was surprised to feel empty as I started ticking off boxes on the list of Things I Want Before I'm 30. Something unexpected happened. The more I accomplished, the less excited I felt. I was paying attention to what everyone was paying attention to, but something didn't add up.

I'm sure you've felt a similar way, because you picked up this book. You're curious to know why you feel empty when you achieve goals you dreamed about for years. You want to know what's wrong with you that you can't enjoy the life you have. You want to know why no matter how much you accomplish, you still feel like you're falling short.

I understand why, and soon you will, too.

I chased everything culture taught me would validate my worth: power, beauty, and status. I got my college degree, exceeded corporate sales targets, got promoted, bought a house, ran a marathon, started a business, paid off my debt, got engaged, rescued a dog, started a podcast, traveled to Europe, bought a Mercedes, moved to L.A., judged the Miss California pageant, released a parody song I wrote with my roommate (stream "Losers in the USA") and now I can add "wrote and published a book" to my list of accomplishments.

All of these items were on my bucket list—and I'm not yet 30. Some are overrated, some underrated, but none of them fixed anything inside me. The one thing that actually brought me peace of mind, happiness, and joy was developing the ability to focus my attention on things I truly value. It was only when I finally stopped chasing the approval of others that I was able to achieve the very last item on my bucket list: inner peace.

I discovered that what I paid attention to consumed my thoughts. My thoughts influenced my actions, and my actions created my life circumstances. On separate occasions, I woke up to find that I was creating life circumstances that did not reflect my values.

I woke up one morning, resenting having to get out of bed to drag myself into the office. *Why am I doing this?* I thought. *I don't enjoy 80 percent of how I spend my time. Something needs to change.*

I woke up one morning, resenting my fiancè for consistently putting his preferences above my needs. *Why am I committed to this person?* I thought. *I don't enjoy 80 percent of how we spend our time. Something needs to change.*

I woke up one morning, resenting my body for not looking toned, firm, and sexy at every angle. *Why am I judging myself so harshly?* I wondered. *I don't enjoy my relationship with my body 80 percent of the time. Something needs to change.*

In order to change my circumstances, I had to take it all the way back to the thought patterns and what grabbed my attention.

Re-evaluating how I measured the worth of my body made the biggest impact on my attention patterns. It's what prompted me to research cultural influence on body image, self-worth related to women's bodies, and start my podcast and body connection coaching business, Confidently She.

Whether it's your career, friendships, relationship, or health, what you're paying attention to most influences how you measure the success of that area of your life.

I wasn't using my values to measure my success; that was the problem. I was using social currency. The amount of attention and approval I got as a result of what I accomplished became how I measured it. Soon, it became how I measured not just my success but also my self worth. The more impressed people were with who I was, the more I liked myself. But eventually, I realized I was building a life for the approval of others, rather than the enjoyment of myself and pursuit of my purpose. This was especially true with my body.

As a conventionally attractive woman, I get attention because of how I look. Growing up getting consistent validation and attention, you don't realize how quickly you get used to it—it's almost as if you're trained to place your value on things other people compliment you on.

"Ugh! Your eyebrows are so perfect."
"You couldn't get fat if you tried."
"I bet you have to beat the boys off with a stick!"
"OMG, you have the perfect butt."
"With that body, you can wear anything."

I heard it all. What's more, I internalized these comments, figuring that my value as a human being was tied to the compliments people gave my physical appearance. Eventually, though, I realized I wasn't giving myself full credit for all of who I was. I was "banking" on my looks too heavily when measuring my self-worth.

I knew something needed to change.

The only way to get started making that change was detoxing from my habit of seeking external approval.

All the external progress, regardless of the category, didn't translate to inner peace the way I thought it would. So, rather than continuing to chase more external progress, I asked myself how it would feel to have peace. Peace is underrated and misunderstood. I used to equate peace with complacency, apathy, or boredom. That's not what it is. Peace comes from the ability to focus your attention on what you can control. Once you know where your attention is going, you have a chance at deciding where it goes next.

So, where's your attention?

Well, you're here. It's happening. You removed all distractions and sat down to focus. You're about to find out just how valuable your attention is—and what's possible when you learn to control it in a meaningful way.

Think about it. At any moment, your phone might light up or ding in an attempt to steal that attention away, and if you're being honest, you like when that happens. It means someone, somewhere wants you. And who doesn't love that? It's exciting to feel wanted. It's meaningful to feel important. It's rewarding to feel essential.

The trouble begins when that feeling of being wanted becomes the goal—when you love that validation too much and start living your life in an attempt to get as much of it as possible. Some call it external validation, but it's more than just that. The amount of attention you get from people validates more than just you as a human being. It socially validates things you like, things you do, and things you believe. And we live in a digital world where you can share those values with millions of people instantly. That kind of instantaneous validation causes an immediate influx of social currency.

Put simply, social currency is the amount of attention you are paid by people in a social setting. The amount of currency you possess changes over time. You are born with some currency, you can earn currency, and you can lose currency. Some people have more at birth than others will ever have in their life. But what exactly does social currency look like?

People pay attention to others for all kinds of reasons. If you're a drop dead gorgeous woman, wearing tight leather head-to-toe, walking through the grocery store, people are gonna notice. If you're a stacked dude, wearing an expensive watch, walking into a bar, people are gonna notice. If you have millions of YouTube subscribers and a Twitter following that rivals Barack Obama, you'll get more attention the moment people find out.

When someone sees you're verified on Instagram, they'll wonder who you are to be important enough for that blue checkmark and probably follow you just because of that. You'll have a high amount of social currency to spend.

When you have social currency, doors open for you with very little effort. Instead of knocking, people let you in without you needing to even touch the handle. That's not to say gaining social currency takes little effort; quite the opposite. If you aren't born with a certain level of beauty, power, or status, it takes a considerable amount of time and attention to accumulate enough to stand out.

When your "social wallet" is full, people listen to you, they trust you, and they want to be close to you. They want to benefit from your social currency. It's the reason you casually mention that Tom Hanks once said, "Hi," to you in the airport. It doesn't get you anything more than the possibility of someone thinking well of you in that moment. (Or you are Tom Hanks and you have more social currency than you know what to do with, so you bend towards being incredibly humble and downplay how impressive you really are to make other people feel comfortable. Loved you in "Big," man.)

But even when you see that glint in their eye or slightly impressed smirk, it doesn't take long before you crave it again. The novelty of attention wears off quickly, so you search for the next thing to make you feel significant. The more difficult the challenge, the longer the satisfaction lasts, but you still end up wondering if it's enough, if it will matter, if anyone really cares about you, or just what you can do for them. If anyone is invested in you, or just the clout that knowing you will bring them.

And therein lies the danger of social currency. You crave it until you have it, and once you have it, you hope people don't see you as a commodity for it. Either way, social currency has your attention, and your life circumstances are built on pursuing more of it or finding people who won't use you for it.

If you want to take control of your attention and no longer be weighed down by whatever social currency you carry, you must understand how social currency works.

As a social creature, you feel safe when people in your life approve of your decisions. You feel like more of a success when your work is recognized and well received. But letting attention lead you down a path towards accumulating social currency is contributing to the rise in anxiety across the globe. Why?

What you need to understand is that social currency itself does not give value beyond the transaction of attention between people. Once the attention is gone, so is the value. I learned this when I qualified for President's Club in my sales role. In the world of large enterprise sales, there's always some form of vacation incentive. When you hit a certain level above your quota, you qualify. You need to do this before the end of the fiscal year. Some quotas are realistic; others are not. I was in a situation where my quota was highly unrealistic—none of my peers were even close to hitting theirs, so qualifying for President's Club felt impossible. The company lowered our quotas in the fourth quarter and gave us a larger territory, but I was still scrapping to get there until the last day of the fiscal year.

I got off the phone with the business owner who would determine my fate. She and her husband were at their cabin in upstate New York for their anniversary. She barely had any signal, but she assured me she would get it signed before the end of the day.

Nearly within the same moment, I closed the last deal in my pipeline to qualify for President's Club. I sighed with exhilaration and relief...then, after about 15 minutes felt a sinking feeling of, "What was all that stress even for?"

My sales director congratulated me. I got a few nice notes from colleagues, but as quickly as that rush of excitement came, it was gone.

The deal was closed, I got the trophy (the trip was cancelled because of COVID, that's a whole other lesson), and nothing material about my day-to-day life changed.

This is why even people with high levels of social currency feel empty when their efforts are not tied to a deeper sense of purpose—because approval of something doesn't increase its value. In other words, attention doesn't equal worth. Everyone can compliment your new hairstyle, but it's still only a hairstyle. It's not going to bring you happiness. Your ex can be jealous of your new relationship, but it doesn't increase the value of that relationship. You can have a large following on Instagram, but it doesn't increase the impact of a post with the caption, "Life is what you make it."

> The things you create need to have value for you beyond the social currency they might create.

This is important because not everyone values social currencies equally. Just like there's an exchange rate for the euro and the USD, there's a social currency exchange rate, which depends on the environment you are spending your social currency in. You could be rich in beauty but poor in power. If you enter into a social setting where power is valued and beauty is not, you will feel a strong sense of inadequacy. You will then believe you need to have power in addition to beauty, and your attention will be directed towards the pursuit of a new social currency.

I'm no stranger to the pull of social validation and living for applause. Thankfully, pattern recognition is one of my strengths. Being an introvert helps with this. When I'm in a new situation, I observe. I look for patterns and notice what they lead to. Then I decide what patterns I'll follow based on the outcomes of each.

Growing up in a small town in southern Minnesota, I didn't want to live an average life. Sure, I wanted the "American Dream," but I wanted it faster than anyone else so I could enjoy it longer—and start dreaming bigger. Money was always important to me. My family was below the poverty line for years until my dad's business took off in the late 90s and early 2000s. With four siblings, I was one of seven people depending on my dad to provide for us. I was 10 when I realized it wasn't normal to do all your shopping at the Salvation Army or have items donated to you directly by people in your church.

My young eyes noticed the pattern shift as our family gained financial independence. The year we went back-to-school shopping at Kohl's, I knew things were different. They were better. I told myself, if nothing else, I would have money when I was older.

I knew I would achieve this goal because in a city with 50,000 people and a graduating class of a few hundred students, it wasn't hard to be at the top of the pack. I wasn't valedictorian, and I didn't get a 36 on my ACT, but I did graduate with a 4.0 without sacrificing my social life, and I got a 25 on my ACT without studying at all. I reminded myself I wasn't trying to get into a bougie Ivy League school. Why would I?

There was a time I considered going to law school. I noticed lawyers made a lot of money and people seemed impressed when they heard that answer to the common question, "What do you do?" But when I looked into it a bit and did the math, it didn't add up. I would need to work way too long and invest way too much money before it would start paying off. I watched my dad make great money working a few hours a day. I wanted that.

I decided to get my education with the least amount of resistance, investment, and trouble so I could get into the business of actually earning a living.

And I did.

I graduated college in three years with only about $20,000 of debt, thanks to scholarships, full course loads, and an incredible program offered in Minnesota called PSEO (Postsecondary Enrollment Options).

My goal was always to start earning money as soon as possible and become financially independent. I didn't care about earning awards along the way. I wanted to climb the corporate ladder and become a respectable "big shot" in the masculine world of tech companies. That's how I could prove myself: by winning a battle rigged for me to lose.

My first "big kid" job was in sales at a cloud software company. Coming out of college, I quickly discovered I didn't know how to actually *do* things. So I searched for patterns to help me not get fired and hopefully get me a raise. It didn't take long before I found one.

Within six months, I was categorized as a top performer and got my first promotion. I felt important. Every time I checked my email, there was a new opportunity for me to prove myself. *Did I get a response? Did they say yes? Am I going to look good in front of my peers?* So, of course, I checked my email every five minutes (or less) so I'd never miss a chance to feel validated in my efforts.

In less than two years, I was promoted twice to a position that took most people five years to land. The rungs on the corporate ladder seemed easy enough to climb.

However, when I turned 23, on track for a six-figure year after my second promotion, I was deeply confused. I wasn't happy. In fact, I was miserable. It didn't make sense. In all the movies, this was the part when the main character would start feeling high all the time. She would float into the office after her promotion, glowing with well-deserved pride, ready to conquer the day. I, on the other hand, was dragging myself into the office, reeking of apathy and ready to call it a day by 2:00 p.m.

I wasn't satisfied with the paychecks, even as they grew. I didn't care about the titles, even as they got more senior. The "floating" feeling faded so quickly. The only time I felt the high of achievement was editing my LinkedIn title and seeing the "Congrats!" and support pour in from colleagues and associates…along with job offers from recruiters as they saw my streak of success. But when the notifications stopped, so did my sense of accomplishment. I didn't want what I had; I wanted the next thing to make people cheer for me.

I got home one night and told my roommate and best friend, Ryan, I didn't understand my job. "The more money I make, the less I care. The more deals I close, the less excited I am. The more senior I get, the less impressed I am with my new title. I'm getting everything I wanted, but now I don't want it."

His response was simple but powerful. "Yeah, it sounds like any progression you make doesn't actually matter to you. The material gain of more money or whatever isn't what you're really after."

So what was I after? I thought I got what I wanted. I hit my six-figure income goal within a few years of graduating from college. I paid off my student loan debt. I was looking at buying a house. Everything was falling into place. I was "crushing it," so why wasn't I happy?

Ryan was right. The pattern didn't make sense because it wasn't aligned with what I valued.

Putting on my analytical, pattern-recognition thinking cap, I did some… digging and developed some analogies to help. If the recipe I followed wasn't giving me the meal I was promised, maybe something was wrong with the ingredients. If the formula wasn't delivering the answer I was promised, something must be wrong with the inputs. I arrived at a dark conclusion. Something must be wrong with ME. Either that, or people were lying, and the pattern wasn't real. The formula didn't actually deliver the results I saw play out in movies.

I saw this in my professional life, personal life, and social life. The "more" I achieved on the surface, the less fulfilled I was on a deeper level. From a social perspective, people saw me "killin' it" but inside I felt like I was the one dying.

Nowhere was this more true than in my relationship with my body. On the outside, I looked good, but mentally I was at war with what I wanted my body to look like versus what it actually looked like.

But you know that. That's why you're here. You're consumed by the drive to do the next thing. To be better, to do more, to make your impact. You want to be significant, but the more progress you make, the more your taste for achievement grows, like some kind of mythical beast who grows back two heads for every one you cut off.

There's an emptiness that comes after achieving something you hoped would give you significance. It's the shallow existence of giving your attention to things in hope of gaining power, status, or beauty.

No matter which social currency you're investing in, trading in, and measuring your worth in, the result is always the same: "This isn't enough. What's wrong with me?"

Don't worry. There's nothing wrong with you (well, at least not because of this). There is, however, something wrong with where your attention and energy is going. You're investing in something that does not give returns.

Nearly everyone does this. The reasons why are different, but the outcome is the same. You spend your life chasing a dream that isn't yours. You give your attention to things you aren't actually interested in. You care what the wrong people think of you. You build an image in order to be accepted, not to be yourself. And when you look back, you feel unfulfilled, like it wasn't worth it…even when what you accomplished is objectively impressive. Even if you accomplished more than your peers. This is the trap of social currency.

It's like keeping all your money in cash. You won't grow your money that way. You will only ever have that amount of money. You can trade it from $100 bills to $5 bills, even to coins and back again, but it will still not give you anything different than money. Over time, the value of that money will decrease with inflation, and its purchasing power will go down. If you attempt to switch currencies and exchange one for another, the exchange rates could eat away at the amount of money you actually have. This is how currency operates.

The same is true when you invest all your attention in social currency. This is the way we transact socially. The influence we carry. How much attention we get. The woman strutting down the street in red-bottom heels, dripped in diamonds, without a wrinkle on her face or hair out of place is getting more attention than the woman wandering in scuffed white sneakers with her hair pulled back under a baseball cap. If you ask each of them where the post office is and they give different answers, whose advice are you going to follow?

Why? Social currency.

You make judgments based on social currency. Every day, all the time. But how you judge depends on your relationship with that currency. How do you value that currency in your social circles?

For example, you might answer, "I trust woman number one. She seems successful and knowledgeable." Another might answer, "I trust woman number two. She seems helpful and honest."

You build social currency by focusing your attention, energy, and effort on accumulating things that increase your power, status, and/or beauty. The only reward you get in exchange for this is social influence. Having social currency gets you attention, which has no intrinsic value. This is why diversifying social currency is the best way to have influence in all social circles, but you must be careful how you invest your attention.

In this book, you'll understand why humans value the "coins" of social currency, why we give attention to the wrong things, and how to live a happy, confident life by paying attention to things that pay relational dividends.

I'm writing this from a place of accumulating certain amounts of different social currencies. No matter the currency or amount, I saw a pattern of diminishing marginal returns. While I, by no means, reached the pinnacle or height of any of these, the pattern helped bring me self-awareness and re-evaluate.

TAKEAWAY

So I want you to stop here for a moment and ask yourself a few questions: When was the last time you felt really good about your life? When was the last time you were at peace? Completely at ease? Let's go the other way. When was the last time you feared you weren't good enough? When was the last time you felt so mentally scattered you didn't know how to actually enjoy your time off? How often do you compare yourself to people and use that as a benchmark for how happy you should be?

If you're anything like I was a few years ago, your answer to this last question is, "Every single day." But it doesn't have to be this way. I'm living proof, and I'm here to show you how.

CHAPTER 2

Beauty, Power, and Status: The Three Social Currencies

Social currency comes in three distinct forms: beauty, power, and status. I want you to think of these like the US dollar, the euro, and the peso. You can transact with each of them in different ways—cash, coin, credit, etc. Each is valued consistently by the country issuing the currency, but there's an exchange rate if you need to trade USD for peso, or peso for euro. You won't get the exact same amount of currency because each are valued differently by different agencies.

The same is true for social currency. People pay attention to different things because they value different things. Either way, the more you pay attention to social currency, the more you want it. But each form has its own distinct advantages and pitfalls.

Beauty

Let's begin with the most volatile currency in the social market. Think Greece in 1986. Think the Philippines in the early 1990s, where inflation was so rampant, the economy nearly collapsed.

If your attention is primarily invested in the social currency of beauty, you'd better have a backup plan, sweetie, because its inflation is out of control.

This currency isn't just relevant to women or physical appearance. The currency of beauty is, in essence, your ability to influence others through desire. This happens in a few different ways. Sex appeal, the desire for the physical pleasure you can create, is an obvious one. Charm—the desire for the physical beauty you create—is another.

Finally, the overlooked coin within the beauty currency: talent. Talent is your ability to create beauty outside of yourself in the world. This includes artists of every kind. You are transacting in beauty currency when you get attention from your music, painting, writing, and everything you use to express that beautiful beating heart of yours.

This is why it's the most enticing, the most rewarding, and—paradoxically—the least satisfying form of social currency. It's enticing because you want to see if your unique form of beauty is accepted and praised. It's rewarding because if your expression of yourself is celebrated, that's more validating than any amount of money in the bank. But it's ultimately the least satisfying because you never know who's going to come along and drag the beautiful thing you created because they're having a bad day and wanted to take it out on you in your YouTube comments.

This fear of painful rejection of your most honest, vulnerable self leads to artists losing sight of their voice or even their muse. They create with doubt instead of boldness. All their music starts sounding the same because they stick with what worked before. The beauty becomes stagnant. It's not truly created; it's replicated.

What started as a genuine expression of yourself can become a feeling of obligation to create what people will like, not what you want to share with the world.

The craving is never long satisfied.

This is especially close to my heart because of my unintentional over-investment in this currency. I didn't realize my self-worth was so heavily invested in my appearance until an ex-boyfriend made me insecure about my body and my entire sense of confidence crumbled.

Before explaining how that happened, I want to start with why it happened in the first place. Our attention as a society is focused on the bodies of women more than, and before, anything else about them. What does that say about what society values? Culturally, we tell women the way they look is equivalent to how much we value them. This is obvious in our marketing campaigns, movie plot-lines, and billion-dollar beauty, weight-loss, and cosmetic surgery industries.

A woman's body is her identity in our current culture. This is a double-edged sword for women. If your body is not valued by culture, your voice isn't heard and you're disrespected—sometimes even oppressed. You aren't given a seat at the proverbial table.

On the flip side, if your body is valued by culture, your voice is heard, but rarely taken seriously. You're given a seat at the table, not because of what you contribute, but because the people already sitting there want to look at you. In other words, you're objectified and ornamental, no matter what other qualities you offer. This cultural pattern creates a framework for how we value ourselves. If culture values your body, so do you. You invest in keeping your body as valuable as possible so you don't lose that social currency you're used to. If culture doesn't value your body, you work like crazy to change your body so you are valued. Either way, where is our focus and attention as women? On our bodies.

For better or worse, paying attention to the social currency of beauty pulls your focus almost entirely on your body. This is why even from a young age girls report feeling insecure about their bodies and having self-conscious thoughts every single day.

This is the problem I address through Confidently She, my podcast and body-connection coaching business. The approach brings the misogyny out of our relationship with ourselves and gives women a path to complete body connection and confidence. Put simply, I fix body image issues. What makes me qualified to teach someone this? Let's get to the story of how my confidence crumbled.

Growing up, I got mostly positive attention for the way I looked. That attention shaped my identity. Positive or negative attention influences how you value the social currency of beauty.

As a kid, you don't know any better than to agree with other people when they say things about you. And when the things they say seem positive and complimentary, why would you ever disagree with that? The problem starts when these compliments start creating the foundation for your identity without you knowing it. Then, when that foundation is questioned or challenged, you have an identity crisis instead of a moment of insecurity.

I was heading into one of the richest seasons of social currency in my young life. It was my senior year of college, where I was known and liked by the faculty. I was set to graduate with high honors in my economics major (nearly impossible). I was training for a marathon and in the best shape of my life. I was preparing for the most competitive year in speech yet. The first few tournaments of the year were a smashing success. I made it to finals in all my categories and even won a few events. This is how I got the attention of a narcissist. (Yes, I was a speech kid. More to come on that later.)

Looking back, I had my pick of guys I could've dated in that season of my life. Talk about missed opportunities. I was a hot commodity in a few social circles, and everyone knew it. I had social currency to spare, but I fell for the narcissist who made me work for his attention, like he was the prize. *Eye roll.* Typical.

At first, he was nothing but impressed with every new detail he found out about me. But within a few short months, this turned to backhanded compliments and outright criticism of the things everyone else seemed to praise me for.

We're talking about beauty, so I'll focus on how he created insecurity and self-consciousness related to my appearance.

First, he compared me to other women, showed me pictures of women he thought were attractive, and made a show of hiding any pictures of his ex because he didn't want to "make me jealous." It was insane—and this is the watered-down version.

If you want the juice, listen to the *Confidently She* podcast episode, When I started becoming aware of my body image. I don't hold back.

After leaving that relationship, I saw how much damage was done to my body image and self-confidence. I didn't know I could crumble like that, and I was afraid I'd never get back to the confident person I used to be. But through that, I realized the old me wasn't truly confident either—she was just blindly benefiting from social currency and mistaking it for confidence. When that currency wasn't valued by someone I cared about, my self-worth folded.

I came back from that all on my own. I developed a framework that built my confidence to a level that is essentially indestructible because it's not based on the opinions of others. It's only based on what I can control and the intentions I have behind the actions I take. I was no longer banking on my looks to boost my confidence. I redefined my body-image philosophy to be completely separate from social currency. That's why the women who join my programs are able to feel confident and connected to their bodies before fixing every single flaw. Because true body confidence can't be based on appearance.

That's the danger of the currency of beauty; it's completely subjective. You can deny the value of it, but also the existence of it. You can say someone isn't beautiful. You can say a work of art is pointless. You can say you "can't stand" the song that's playing. This makes beauty a volatile, dangerous, risky investment to pursue.

> When the currency you value can be devalued and denied, it's an identity crisis waiting to happen.

Power

The original form of social currency is as caveman as it gets. The tallest, strongest man was seen as the best, most desirable mate. I'm sure his wife let him get away with leaving dirty socks strewn across the bedroom floor—or cave, rather because, what's she going to do, leave? Physical stature and strength is the first primitive form of this currency. People make assumptions about tall, muscular men with a full head of hair to this day; whether or not they're attractive is a separate thing entirely.

Height covers a multitude of a man's sins; somehow, we haven't let evolution work this one out of our system. People like tall men. They also like strong men, but not too strong (here's where you start seeing the annoying problem that's 10x'd in the beauty currency).

You see men going to great lengths to show their strength if they have it and hide their weakness if they don't. My ex fiancé had such a strength complex. He wasn't a tall guy, but he was small-town famous for having a six pack since sixth grade. At one point, he got into bodybuilding and fitness competitions. This was before we got together—I'm not into that kind of thing. He put on muscle, got the spray tans, and ate nothing but watered-down oats and bland chicken for weeks. Or so I'm told.

When he gave up the competition lifestyle—thank God—he naturally lost some strength and muscle definition. The six pack stuck around. When we got together, I started getting back into running shape and working out, but he was resisting going to the gym. Or he wanted to go alone. I didn't understand. Didn't he used to live for this? We lived together, and it just made sense to go at the same time. Excuses kept coming every time I had my gym bag waiting by the front door. Being an independent Scorpio, I went without him.

Eventually, I was sick of paying for our gym membership when he didn't use his share (a glimpse into what the relationship became before I called off the wedding).

"If there's a reason you're not going to the gym for a while, just tell me. Otherwise, it doesn't make sense for me to keep paying for something you never use."

The truth came out after an awkward silence when he realized I wasn't saying more until he did.

"I can't lift like I used to," he admitted.

My face turned into a scrunched, inverted smile and my eyes got wide as they darted sharply to the side. It's a really cute expression I make every time I'm genuinely confused. It's like a gag reflex or my crush on Charlie Puth—I don't know when it started; I just wish it would go away.

"Okay," I said.

Then it clicked. I spoke more softly this time.

"Wait…are you not going to the gym because you don't want the confirmation that you're not as strong as you were when you worked out twice a day…five days a week?"

I was hoping he would see how unrealistic that expectation was, but instead he seemed legitimately embarrassed. Not for the reason I saw. He should've been embarrassed that he was expecting his body to be at the same level of strength as when he was obsessively training. That's what I would be embarrassed by. But he was actually embarrassed, or even ashamed, that he wasn't as strong as he was before.

He wasn't giving himself an ounce of grace or practicality to the expectation he placed on himself. He wanted to think of himself as strong, and this would prove that he wasn't at his strongest. What bothered me most was he was actually still very strong by most people's standards. He just chose to use the highest point he reached as his measuring stick, setting himself up to fail. Poor guy.

Though he didn't realize it, this guy was trying to make up for what felt to him like a devastating loss of power. He felt like his social wallet—once chock-full, thanks to his pumped-up biceps—was now growing thin. It didn't matter that he was technically still strong because he *perceived* himself to be weak and therefore less worthy of other people's attention. In other words, he felt socially poor relative to his former self.

This is incredibly common. We compare ourselves to the highest point we reached, not to what's realistic based on our current habits and lifestyle. If you want to make progress, you need to be realistic, not harshly comparing your "best self" with your current self. That's not fair.

Ironically, whether or not a tall, strong guy actually *does* anything with his height and strength is irrelevant; he gets points just for having it. Case in point, my ex liked the feeling of having the option to exercise (no pun intended) his strength, even though actually taking that option would prove he was wrong.

Power can take many forms, and one of them—arguably the most relevant to our capitalist society—is money. Wealth gives you incredible power in the sense that you can have things most people can't. You get to make the decisions. You get to call the shots. In the previous story, I was wielding the power of the gym membership. I was paying for it, so I got to decide if we kept it or cancelled.

When you have money, you don't even have to use it in order to influence others and transact your social currency. When people know you're rich, they treat you differently, for better or worse. They can be sucking up to you or cursing you under their breath, but either way, they're thinking about you. They know you have the power to make their dreams come true or—if the whim strikes you—to ruin their future. In other words, you have control.

But before you walk away thinking that control and wealth are one and the same, check your assumptions. Certainly people who have wealth can also have a high amount of control, but it's not always the case. Look no further than everyone's favorite binge show, *The Office*. Michael Scott did not have considerable strength, stature, or wealth, but he was in control of the office, and that gave him power. He decided who worked on weekends, went home early, or got their bathrobe from corporate taken away when there weren't enough to go around.

Though power can come in many forms—money, control, even brute strength—it's not in the exercising of power that social currency comes; it's in the option to exercise it.

Status

When investing in social currency, Status is precious metals and real estate. You can pretty much bet it will hold its value in the long term. It's a safe bet, but you're not gonna get rich quick off it. Changes in value of this currency happen slow enough for you to keep up and pivot alongside it.

The first coin in the status currency is relationship. This is a coin that is slowly reversing how it's valued. We used to highly respect and approve of anyone with a wedding ring on their finger, especially if that person was married with kids. Even your car insurance rate goes down when you get married, implying that you're now a more responsible adult who won't be rolling through stop signs or running red lights anymore. (State Farm should meet some people I went to high school with; marriage changes nothing.)

Even my married friends would be the first to admit that being married does not magically bring someone into a higher level of consciousness. Still, there's a certain level of respect that married people have for other married people. I have a hunch it's because their life is fixed, meaning stationary and decided. It makes people uncomfortable to be around someone who's free and has choices when your future is set in stone in a big way. But because many people of marrying age were raised by divorced or single parents, we're seeing people put off getting married.

What we're seeing now is a shift to valuing singleness, especially in men, and slowly seeing the beginnings of valuing it in women.

Marriage seems to be the ultimate achievement for a woman and the ultimate compromise for a man. Within singleness, there's still a level of relationship status. Are you seeing anyone? You should be. This fickle currency doesn't even know what it wants, especially from women. If you're single, you need to do it the right way; otherwise, you're clearly "desperate for a man" and no one wants you.

> Relationship status is a fickle form of social currency because each person you encounter will value your relationship status differently. In one group you might have pressure to settle down and get married, while in another you'd be seen as a social outcast and a "traditionalist" for doing the exact same thing.

The next couple of coins in the social currency of status are brands and associations. Here you can even think sport teams or country clubs. How we associate with brands places us in a social status. In my hometown, people talked about Ford versus Chevy and which truck was better. It made me want to barf. I cannot think of a more pointless topic to debate, but I heard it constantly. I'm not proud to admit I even participated in it, but only to offer that the Ford logo was a lazy brand expression so my preference was obviously Chevy on account they used gold and actually made an effort at creativity.

The brands that truly designate social status, in my opinion, are in fashion. Your choices in this area set you apart and say something about who you are. Do you have a YSL bag from Nordstrom or shop at TJ Maxx for Kate Spade? What brands do you wear? What do you represent?

Back when I was growing up in the Midwest, I thought brands like Coach and Michael Kors represented the height of fashion and sophistication. That's because I was in small-town USA and I had no idea what else was really out there. I wasn't paying attention to it very much. But when I moved to L.A., I began to see new designers everywhere. I realized just how cheap and commoditized the brands I grew up with had become, and I decided to swap them out for lesser known brands like Dita, Alice + Olivia, Fiorucci, and others. Some of these fashion brands function almost like a dog whistle to certain high-status segments of the population. Case in point, when I put on my $600 Dita sunglasses, I know that 90 percent of people won't have any idea what they are or how much they cost, but the other 10 percent will and that's the 10 percent I'd like to talk fashion with. (All that aside, they're SO comfortable. Seriously. Can't even feel them on my face.)

Fashion brands aren't the only ones that matter, of course. Which coffee do you get, Starbucks or Dunkin'? (I'm at Starbucks when I'm out of the house, but it's Dunkin' all day for my Kurig.) What kind of car do you drive, a Mercedes Benz or a Subaru? (Would your answer change if I offered a used five-year-old Mercedes Benz versus a brand-new Subaru?)

> The brands we choose to align ourselves with project a certain image about us—whether we want them to or not. This image is a form of social currency.

Finally, the most reliable coin in the status social currency is institutions. Which governing bodies have approved of you? Where did you graduate high school? College? Do you have an MBA or PhD? Are you certified? Licensed? Recognized? Decorated? Validated by someone other than yourself who will vouch to the world that you're worth something?

When you have institutional validation bolstering your status social currency, you're pretty much guaranteed to impress people. This is why you see "NYT Best-Selling Author" "Harvard Ph.D." "3X Grammy Winning Producer" in digital profiles. Before you know anything else about this human being, they want you to respect them. What you actually respect is the institution. That institution has validated this person with an achievement, so the respect usually transfers, even if it's not merited.

We respect these status markers in others and crave them for ourselves, but do they actually matter? Well, they can, but a lot of the time they don't. This is because status can be exchanged with the social currency of power. We saw that clearly with the scandal of 2019 when it was leaked that wealthy families bought their children's way into prestigious universities. I think we all had the suspicion, but it makes you reconsider what you're impressed by when the illusion of merit is shattered before your eyes.

We also see examples of extremely capable, intelligent, talented people finding success without receiving formal education or institutional validation. Kendra Scott dropped out of Texas A&M and later used $500 to start a company currently valued over $1 billion. Hans Zimmer composes scores for countless blockbuster films with no formal technique or music education. Some of the most respected, talented, and tenured actors have yet to win an Academy Award including Glenn Close, Bradley Cooper, Amy Adams, Sir Ian McKellen, Winona Ryder, Robert Downey Jr., and Harrison Ford. Clearly, institutional endorsement or vali-dation is not a necessary component of success or talent.

I have peers and friends who secretly doubt if they're any good because they don't have a degree or certification in their given line of work. Which I think is the dumbest thing in the world. (This is different from gaining formal education because you value learning, I'll cover that later.)

If you're good at what you do, why do you need to spend time and money for an institution to vouch for you? This line of thinking leads quickly to imposter syndrome. I don't have a certification for body image coaching or a background in psychology, yet my approach is helping thousands of women heal their relationship with their body, grow friendships, strengthen marriages, and ignite careers. The important thing is learning to judge yourself and others not based on what institutions have given their stamp of approval, but based on an informed mixture of effort, intention, and results.

TAKEAWAY

Certifications, degrees, or awards from institutions may inflate your social currency by giving you perceived credibility, but are not a necessary component of true credibility.

CHAPTER 3

Attention as a Limited Resource

The things we're told will bring happiness, confidence, and fulfillment are not bad things. Power, beauty, and status are useful
and valuable, but they are not what will satisfy your relational
and social desires. They are not a catch-all for insecurity. And
everything comes with a cost. You need to understand what
you're investing in before continuing to give it the only asset
you cannot save. Attention.

Attention is interesting. It's something you can't create. You also
cannot save attention the way you can save energy or time. You
cannot be more efficient with your attention. You have a constant
stream of attention given to your conscious mind. Some forms
of meditation teach you to harness your attention onto nothing,
but even then, you're still directing it somewhere (into a void).
Here's the thing, your consciousness will always go *somewhere*,
but where it goes is up to you.

Attention is attention spent.

It doesn't matter if it's attention you invested in a relationship
or attention you invested in habitually checking your work

email. Attention can be quantified, captured, and put to work for you—or drained away from you and into something that isn't important at all. But either way, it's always going somewhere. So whether you respond to that text message and divert your attention away from this page, or keep your attention here, it's streaming constantly.

Of course, you might be thinking, *Well, Rebekah, if I can pay attention to people, people can also pay attention to me. Isn't that getting it back?* Not exactly. That attention is worth something (that's what most of this book is about), but you aren't getting *your* attention back. Think of it this way; if one hundred people are paying attention to you, you cannot pay attention to one hundred things as a result. It does not add to your capacity for attention in any given moment. You can still only pay attention to a few things at once, when divided, or one thing, when focused.

If attention is a resource, it is a limited resource. Certainly it can be redistributed, but it can never multiply. This means that when you're paying attention to something, it's at the expense of another thing. Think of it like money. Money spent on food cannot be money spent on clothing. You can buy both, but you need enough money for both. If you don't have enough to cover the cost, you can buy all of one, all of the other, or settle for half of each, knowing full well you're not getting the amount you initially wanted for that price.

Attention functions the same way. You're literally paying attention to things, people, and ideas all day long. You can split your attention, but then no one thing gets all of it. Your divided attention is sometimes enough for simple tasks, but the more your attention is divided in relationships and meaningful projects, the more they will suffer.

If you're thinking, *Rebekah, stop depressing me!* I have some good news for you. You get to choose where your attention goes. This includes who or what gets full or partial attention, and why. The trouble comes when you're unaware of how that attention is being spent. Our attention, when uncontrolled, often leads us towards things that bring attention back to ourselves. This is why social media is popular; it's an opportunity for people to give us attention. It's an opportunity for us to look good. This inclination towards instant gratification or a quick fix creates a cyclical demand. You give attention to something hoping to get more attention back. Rinse. Repeat.

Unfortunately, this cycle is flowing in the wrong direction. In order to build the type of social wealth that pays dividends, you need to put attention into assets that bring real fulfillment, not just social currency. For example, things that facilitate health, connection, expression, creativity, and growth. When you have these "life assets," you have the freedom to enjoy any social currency coming in as a result because you know there's something truly valuable creating that currency. It's not transactional.

If you're struggling to feel secure in your social standing, your friendships, relationships, etc., take a look at what you're paying attention to. What you pay attention to influences your values. If you're constantly paying attention to your notifications, weight, follower count, number of events you're invited to, money in the bank, etc., you're valuing social currency more than you're valuing your life assets.

The amount of attention you get in a given day, week, or year is your spending social currency. The strange thing about social currency is that it doesn't matter if what you're doing is unique, impactful, or uplifting. Social currency only cares about if people are watching. It doesn't matter if what you're saying is true, helpful, or wise; social currency is only gained if people are listening. You could be 100-percent wrong, spreading anxiety-inducing information across the internet, and have enormous numbers of views, likes, comments, and—therefore—social currency.

I remember during the 2016 Presidential Election, I got the first serious wake up call about how reading and watching news coverage impacted my mental health. I constantly felt anxious. I felt powerless when I thought about my fears coming true. I just wanted it to be over. But even after the results were announced, the anxiety continued. I realized I was the one allowing this stress in my life. Yes, it was a politically charged time in American history, but I was giving my attention to it. I was allowing it to disrupt my inner peace. So I decided to stop paying attention that stress. I refused to give social currency to the chaos, fueling the fire of my fears. I unfollowed, unsubscribed, and unfriended. I decided to pay attention to the things that wouldn't change no matter who was elected president and the things I had control over. Within a matter of days, the anxiety lifted. I was free, not because I got the outcome I wanted or because people stopped talking about it, but because I took back control over my attention.

The same is true for you. You can choose to let your attention go to the highest bidder, or you can invest it in something that will bring you peace. Either way, again, you're always paying attention to something; it's time to make it work for you.

It's important to remember that the attention you can give in a day is a limited, finite resource. However, the attention you can receive (your social currency) is practically unlimited with today's digital platforms. This mechanism of social currency and influence is powerful. It's the reason influencers make millions. When people pay attention to you, they are essentially saying they're willing to give their attention to whatever you're giving attention to. For example, a brand pays $10,000 to a beauty blogger who posts a video talking about how he uses their skincare products to achieve smooth, clear skin (social currency of beauty, by the way) This money is maximized because his attention for 10 minutes is multiplied by his hundreds of thousands of followers.

The social currency of this man multiplies his attention to a product, translating to hundreds of thousands of "attention units" paid to this item. Every person who views the video is paying attention to what he's paying attention to. He's harnessing his social currency. If he loves the creative outlet of beauty products and health benefits of skincare, he probably feels fulfilled by paying attention to this project. If he's solely doing these brand partnerships for the money and the "likes," it's likely this exchange of social currency isn't fulfilling—for long.

TAKEAWAY

While the attention you can receive is infinite, the attention you can give is limited, so choose your focus intentionally. Cautious people pay attention to what they fear. Courageous people pay attention to what they desire.

CHAPTER 4

Learning to Recognize Attention Patterns

Each day you spend a little attention here, a little there. Over the course of a month, your life progresses down the path your daily attention spending paves for you. Looking back over years and decades, a pattern slowly emerges. Here are stories of three people and where their attention patterns got them.

Making Dad Proud

Breanna has worked every single weekend since dropping out of college. Building a business takes time, and she's not going to fail. Her dad built a highly profitable software business from scratch after dropping out of college, and she remembers as a young girl hearing her brother asking who was going to take over the family business. Her dad replied, "As soon as one of you builds your own company and takes it public, you can come work for me."

She takes her friends' joke about being "married to her business" as a compliment to her work ethic. It's a source of pride for Breanna. But her father's words echo in her mind every time she gets invited to a weekend vacation or even a night out with friends. She's determined to be the kid who takes her company public. She's made up her mind to get the family business. She's going to be the one to make her dad proud. So, with a little pang of regret, she declines the invitations from friends and focuses on work.

Breanna spends the next year working 75-hour weeks, taking a break only to return home and collapse in her bed for four hours. She works as hard as she can to make her dad proud, giving up all the people and things she loves along the way.

And it pays off. She has a successful business. But she doesn't understand the empty feeling that creeps in at the end of each day.

As she combs through a pile of documents on her desk, a notebook falls out. She picks it up and flips through it to see if it's worth keeping. It's filled with lyrics and chords she wrote back in a songwriting class she took before dropping out of college. Breanna's dream was to be an artist. She was a talented musician, but her dad told her it wasn't practical. He convinced her she wasn't good enough to make money and that having a business was the best way to ensure security for her future. It's been eight years since she thought about that class. She begins to pick out a melody, humming quietly to herself as she remembers that moment when music came alive in her soul.

Finally, the day arrives that she's been dreaming about for years. She's about to take her company public and can't wait to tell her dad the news. As soon as it's official, she calls him up to let him know. She can practically hear the grin in his voice as he tells her, "You can come work for me any time."

In the car ride home from the office, she's coming off of the high of reaching her goal and the familiar empty feeling sinks in as strongly as it did before. She drives in silence while tears slip down her cheeks.

Sacrificing for the Scale

The 5:00 a.m. alarm blares as Les groans. She went to bed the night before in her workout clothes so that she'd be obligated to get to the gym this morning—one of the many "health hacks" she's posted on her Instagram. Fitness is her life, and she has over 800,000 followers to "show up" for.

Growing up, her dad used to make her waffles for breakfast—her favorite food in the whole world. She doesn't eat them anymore because they have too many calories, so instead she chokes down a green smoothie before leaving for her 5:30 a.m. HIIT class. Tracking calories is easy because of the apps; her Apple watch monitors her activity, so she always knows if she's hitting her goals for the day. Every time she walks past the Waffle Stop on her way to work, she stops and takes a deep breath in through her nose, knowing she's making the right choice by saying "no."

As she settles into her day, she mentally tracks how many calories she'll eat for lunch. She has a date that night, and she probably will have a drink or two. As she skims the menu for dinner, it's not looking like lunch is in the cards. Around 3:30 p.m., she's starving as her co-workers invite her to take off a bit early for happy hour.

She can't stop thinking about the leftover tacos she has at home and knows if she goes to happy hour, there's no way she can go through with this date.

Yeah, I'll finish up here and catch up with you in a bit! she lies. She's going to go home and have a taco before her date later. After finishing three tacos, tortilla chips with guac, and a glass of white wine, she looks at her calorie tracker, feeling a rush of guilt.

Jeez, I could've had waffles for breakfast…

After a disgusted look at herself in the mirror, she texts Jay, asking to reschedule. Beauty is pain, though; if she doesn't keep her figure, guys aren't going to want to date her in the first place. She puts on Netflix, opens Instagram, and smiles at the 3,560 likes on her latest gym selfie.

Making Up for a Shortcoming

Ali is a smart guy. Growing up, he was bullied for being short, so he's always felt the need to prove himself in other ways—a classic Napoleon complex. Somewhere along the way, he turned his fixation with external validation into a constant quest for achievement. Every few years he sets his sights on a new "height" he wants to reach, namely degrees from prestigious universities. Sometimes he finishes them. Sometimes, he gets "bored," realizes he's "actually too smart for this subject," and changes his mind.

He considers law school, business school, and medical school trajectories, each with PhDs in addition to the required degrees for employment after graduation. All are paths that would validate his intellect and ability to lead. As the years go on, he accumulates accreditations like stamps in his passport. Finally, he reaches his desired height when he graduates with high honors from an Ivy League school, "just as many had predicted."

In the waiting room before taking his boards, he runs into another guy, who asks him what he would be doing if he wasn't a doctor. He replies, "I don't know. Who knows what could have happened?" But after just six months in residency, Ali loses all interest in not only work but every daily activity. The program is much harder than he expected. He's used to tests and courses, but the actual work of being a resident physician turns out to be thankless, messy, and frustrating.

"I want to be a doctor, but this sucks!" he says one night on the way home from work, anxious, frustrated, and feeling more like a fraud than ever. Yet he doesn't know how to get off the path, so he keeps showing up every day, going through the motions, until finally the residency ends. He receives his white coat, designating him a full fledged physician—the pinnacle of everything he's been working toward.

Ali has reached the end of his path, but something inside of him feels broken. He still feels like less of a man than he thinks he should be. So he types "Harvard MBA" into a Google search, determined to chase a true sense of accomplishment.

Unintentional Investments

These three stories illustrate people unintentionally investing in each of the three types of social currency—power, beauty, and status, respectively. To their dismay, they discovered that these investments did not actually enrich their lives. So why did they still feel so committed to the paths they were on? Why was it so hard for them to direct their attention elsewhere, to something in their lives they would find more fulfilling?

Simple. Because we are wired to pay attention to what other people pay attention to. If everyone suddenly turned to look out the window, you would do the same thing. Your brain thinks, *There must be something important out that window; otherwise, no one would be looking.* In many cases, you might be correct. But when the thing everyone is looking at is a video of two girls and one cup…you have to ask yourself, *Why am I watching this? I don't care if everyone else is talking about it or watching it. I'm not going to.*

We also—unfortunately—have a tendency to like whatever other people like. We want to be included, and that means knowing about what other people know about. It takes courage to like what you truly like without being influenced by other people. Being introduced to new things and growing as a person because of the people you know is different from letting yourself be influenced in an attempt to gain social currency.

An easy way to test this is to ask yourself a series of questions:

1. If no one else knew I was doing this, would I still do it?
2. If I were alone, would I watch this (movie, YouTube video, etc.)?
3. Am I doing this because I enjoy it, or because I think people will be impressed when they hear about it?

After doing this for a while, you start feeling a difference in your body when you do things you like versus when you do things because other people like them. I'm not talking about deferring to your sister's restaurant preference when she comes for a visit or skipping a happy hour with coworkers because your partner needs help prepping for a work event. Short-term self-sacrifice is an important part in investing in long-term growth. Again, it's important to not be selfish and only do what you like, but you must be careful not to lose yourself in other people to gain their approval. This is when selflessness becomes long-term self-sacrifice. Of course, I'm not saying the line is always obvious. In fact, it's often blurry. But a good first step is to make sure you have a solid foundation of what is you and what isn't you. Develop clear boundaries with yourself and make sure they are consistent in your relationships. (Easier said than done, I know, but I never promised you any of this would be easy!)

Earlier I told you attention is valuable. It's actually getting more valuable as the digital world expands. This is a simple rule of economics (my major in college). Supply and demand. The number of things easily available for us to give attention to is at an all-time high, and it continues to grow. There are five hundred hours of video content being uploaded to YouTube per minute. As you scroll through Instagram, there are 64,440 posts added per minute. Netflix alone released over 60 original, English-speaking feature films in 2020, a year the film industry slowed to a near halt. Which is insane compared to the 371 total movies released in the United States and Canada in 2000.

We have a constant stream of attention, but it is a limited resource because our *time* is limited. There are opportunity costs. You can't pay attention to everything. The supply of things to look at is growing, and the amount of attention we can give is staying the same. In other words, there is an increase in competition within the supply, and the demand for attention is growing. In case you've never taken an economics class, let me break it down for you: When the supply of a product increases and the demand does not increase, it results in a price decrease of that product. This is one reason technology becomes less expensive over time. More manufactures enter the market, creating competition between manufacturers. More companies want the consumer demand and they're willing to accept a lower price to capture market share. The demand (in this case, people's attention) becomes more valuable.

As attention becomes more valuable and the competition for your attention grows, it becomes more difficult to manage. New apps and advertisements are designed to capture your attention and hold it. If you're not careful, you open TikTok in the morning before work and an hour later, you realize you still haven't showered or eaten breakfast (speaking from personal experience). Or you wake up and see an email notification from work that leads you from your bed to your desk without having a chance to center yourself or set intentions for the day. Before you know it, it's 5:30 p.m., and you didn't get anything done you actually wanted to.

That is attention wasted. Even if you did technically get something done, it wasn't the thing you wanted to get done. You're not alone in this feeling of powerlessness in the face of what vies for your attention.

When you're not in control of your attention, a few things happen. In the micro sense, your energy is drained at the end of every single day and it doesn't feel like you're making progress, even though you're exhausted. In the macro sense, your life is spent pursuing varying achievements in hope of getting enough social currency to satiate your need for significance.

You aren't actually building life assets. Taking control of your attention allows you to direct it towards things you care about, not just accolades or progress for the sake of progress. You'll attract relationships with depth and meaning, not just someone who looks good enough to validate your ego when you walk into a room with them.

The hollow feeling I had after getting that promotion was because I was doing it for the social currency of power. I didn't actually value the career I was pursuing. I wasn't using that social currency for anything more than accumulating more. The more I did things for attention, the deeper the desire grew because now that I had attention, I feared I would lose it.

The reason you care so much what other people think is because you pay attention to what people think. But by the end of this book, you'll be investing attention in social and relational assets that are worth so much to you, they make the concept of trading currency irrelevant. You will learn to pay attention to the right things for you.

Before you can invest your attention, you need to stop any attention leaks. It's like creating a financial budget. The first step to saving money is to stop mindless spending. Over the next few chapters, you'll learn why you aren't properly budgeting attention, and you'll get steps to start doing it properly. You need to know where it's going before you can make changes. It starts with finding your patterns.

Action Steps

Your attention is valuable, so you need to do what you can to protect it. Start with your phone.

1. Turn off social, news, and email notifications. This will protect your attention from being disrupted when you're on and off your phone.

2. Turn off screen notifications, sounds, and badges. The goal is for your phone to stop bothering you. Put yourself in full control of when and how you find out you have an email or social notification. Having your badges turned off removes the sense of anticipation of what could be waiting for you. This is distracting, too, because if you open your phone to pull up an email and see that little red circle hovering over Instagram, you start thinking, *Oooh, I wonder what's waiting for me on Instagram.* All you're doing is letting those red circles have a disproportionate amount of influence over your emotions, actions, and motivations.

3. Consider using the "Screen Time" tool to track your social media usage and phone usage in general. Breaking free from any pattern requires you to see the pattern in the first place, and if you're anything like me, you may be surprised to find just how much of your attention you're spending on various apps.

TAKEAWAY

Here's the thing, the more freedom you give to the pings and beeps and vibrations coming from the device in your pocket, the less control over your attention you have. So turn them off. No lighting up, no sounds, no badges. This protects your attention and allows you to be in control of what and who gets your attention, how they get it, and when you give it.

CHAPTER 5

The Trap of Insta-Validation

It feels good to be liked. Even when I'm not into a guy, it's nice to flirt and feel attractive now and then. It provides a little dose of temporary happiness. Whether it's for a few fleeting moments or entire days where nothing goes wrong, we're all working towards a happier version of ourselves. It's mostly found in simple things. Showing up to the DMV and being the only one in line: happiness. Your Friday afternoon meeting pushed out to next week: happiness. Noticing the cute stranger smiling at you from across the bar: happiness.

No matter how often you feel this way, it's worth paying attention to the nature in which it usually comes. Happiness is found in the absence of pain or the presence of pleasure. If you're in a season of pain, lowering that by any amount will bring happiness. I remember when I was going through the worst breakup of my life, if someone made me laugh, I considered it a good day. The bar was low.

If you're in a painless season, the only way to bring happiness is by adding pleasure. Laughing is no longer enough to make it a good day. You need something especially good to happen to make an impact on your happiness. Your baseline of happiness increases when you don't experience pain frequently—which is a good thing. But the difference, the delta, of pain versus pleasure is always the measure for what makes you happy. This delta moves around as your life gets more and less painful.

This is why we have "first-world problems." Think about it. The first paycheck you got was incredible. You got money to go buy things. Now, getting paid is expected and it takes a lot of money to make you feel excited when you see the direct deposit show up in your bank account.

That's a first world problem, but it's not a conscious choice. It's your ability to adapt to your surroundings. Wherever you are, you adapt, and your expectations adjust accordingly. You develop a tolerance for whatever you're routinely exposed to. Thankfully, you're living in a time where you're regularly exposed to good things. Your basic human needs are easily met. You have food, water, and protection from reasonable harm. You expect that. You expect it to a point where if you don't have food immediately when you want it, you get irritated and cranky. Your privilege can make you soft.

The feelings of guilt set in quickly. Even observing the stress factors of my life makes me feel privileged beyond belief. Am I really stressing over how soon to book my vacation to Mexico? When I first had this realization, before it occurred to me how social currency influenced my happiness, I couldn't help but wonder why I wasn't happier. All my needs were met, so why wasn't it enough? It's not like I had "real" problems.

But problems, pain, and pleasure are all relative. Your problems are real to you. Your pain is real to you. Your pleasure is real to you. And everyone is living their life, trying to balance their personal happiness equation in their favor. You shouldn't deny your own pain because someone else has it worse. You shouldn't deny your own happiness because someone else has it better.

But once we pass into the "first world problems" section of the happiness tolerance spectrum, in which nearly all of us presently sit—iPhone in hand—something as a culture shifts. Our happiness tolerance is so high that we need the absence of pain, the presence of pleasure, and the ultimate sweetener to any happiness—getting it approved by other people. The more the better.

Getting a new car is great. You'll feel happy for a while just from the simple act of smelling the fresh leather. But posting "I did a thing..." with a picture of your new car on Facebook and getting hundreds of people to "like" that you got a new car is like happiness on ecstasy. You were already having fun, but this made it ten times better.

Being exposed to that kind of validation changes your behavior. Experiencing that consistently over an extended period of time makes you expect the ecstasy version of happiness. When you get engaged, it's not really about the engagement anymore—it's about how many people "like" that you got engaged. It's not enough to get a new house; you want to get a better house than the one your cousin moved into last year. Now it's not enough to only get the new car; you want people to applaud you for doing it. This is the progression of human nature when exposed to social currency at this level for an extended period of time. When people clap for you, you also adapt to that and want more. But where can that come from?

Personally, I caught myself deeply relishing the moments where I could show off to people who didn't like me. They say the best revenge is living well, and now we have a way to show everyone just how well we're living (even if it's rented...they'll never know).

On that same note, if you're honest, and anything like me, a shameful piece of you likes it when someone is envious that you "did a thing" and people like it. It's not something I'm proud of and I've kicked the habit for the most part, but man, it feels great to make the haters jealous.

You're a calculated person. We all are. You measure what you think you're going to get when you invest time and attention in certain things. You carefully select the "thing" you want to do.

"It's not worth it" is something you say when the expected payoff is less than the effort required. Whether it's financial, physical, or social, you want a return on your investment. This is why there's an emptiness when you reach the end point of a goal, even a big goal, if the main payoff you expect is praise in the form of a few hundred (thousand) "likes" or back-to-back phone calls congratulating you on your success.

That lasts a few minutes, maybe a few days, and then you're right back to where you started, trying to find the next thing to bring the attention back and prove your worth all over again. It's a pattern I noticed in myself. It's something you can break. It's not how you have to keep living your life.

By now, you know there are three avenues for getting social currency. You can get it through power, beauty, and status (PBS, an easy way to remember). You also know people focus their attention on getting social currency, often at the expense of what they truly value. We do this because we are social creatures wanting to be accepted. We long for significance, and our fickle hearts quickly forget that we have it and desire more. Social currency gives us an "easy" way to feel significant, even for a few minutes. It's easy in the sense that you can use your social currency to get attention and validation in a few seconds if you post a picture on Instagram.

More like, Insta-validation. Insta-attention. Insta-comparison. I could keep going... I'll stop.

The more social currency you have, the more things compete for your attention. When you have people bidding for your attention, it makes you feel important. You get used to monitoring the auction, getting paid (social currency, of course) by the winners, and looking forward to the next thing that wants your attention. Eventually, the more attention you get, the more of it you need to feel important. When you enjoy watching the bidding, it hurts when you notice it slow down or stop.

Where humans used to be content with and entirely focused on simple needs like food and shelter, civilization has evolved to where it doesn't take much time to get that. So, you look for the next thing to focus on, not because you need more but because your attention must go somewhere. It looks for ways to improve, expand, and explore. When used correctly, focusing this surplus of attention can lead to beautiful forms of creativity, self-expression, and unique opportunities to connect deeply with people you love.

But if you're not careful, what can happen instead is that it feeds into itself. Your attention goes towards things that will get you attention, for better or worse—and often it's for worse.

Social Currency and Poor Behavior

There is a direct correlation in our culture between social currency and poor behavior. In general, the more social currency you have, the more society tolerates inconsistent moral standards and character flaws. You can see this correlation in the following graph:

Social Currency Tolerance

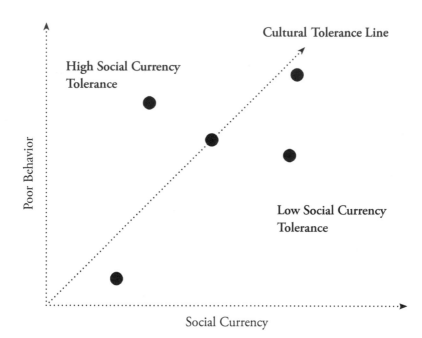

If someone exhibits high amounts of poor behavior, they need equally high social currency to not feel the impact a "normal" person would. Simple examples of this include sex scandals where a high-profile man gets little to no cultural, financial, or reputational consequences and, hey, maybe even a term in the White House. Men, in general, are given more leeway in our culture when it comes to bad behavior. We tend to be much more willing to forgive men than women for the same bad choices, whether infidelity or otherwise. Why? Because in any patriarchy, men automatically have higher social currency than women, particularly power and status.

The important thing to understand is that YOUR personal tolerance line can be different from the mainstream cultural tolerance line, and YOU get to set its position.

Take a look:

Social Currency Tolerance

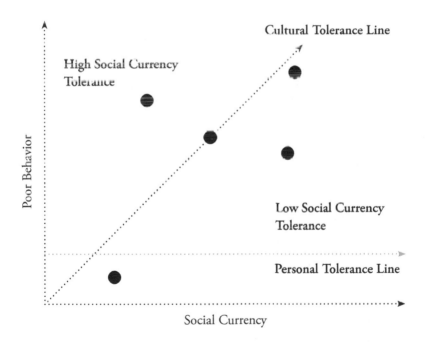

The lower your tolerance line, the higher your self-worth is. If you have a very low sense of self-worth and confidence, your tolerance for poor treatment will be very high because you're desperate for people to accept you. This is especially true if the people you're with have more social currency than you and you want to benefit from being around them.

If your little dot on this graph appears above the cultural tolerance line, that means you have a high social currency tolerance. If your dot is below that line, you have a low social currency tolerance relative to the mainstream cultural tolerance level. Make sense? Your goal should be to set your personal tolerance line as low as possible and make sure it stays the same regardless of your circumstances.

It's worth noting that some people's tolerance lines are vertical rather than horizontal. This happens when they decide they're only willing to accept people at a certain level of social currency. In other words, their tolerance is based on social currency rather than behavior. It probably goes without saying, but if you count yourself in this category, this book is going to expose the shallow nature of your values, and probably piss you off. But here's the thing, I'm here to help solve a problem, and that starts by exposing it—which can hurt.

If you weren't an economics major like me, and you don't like graphs, I'll boil down this concept for you into one simple sentence: the less crap you tolerate from people—regardless of how much social currency they have—the higher your own self-worth. That's not to say you cut people out of your life at the first sign of trouble. But if you start noticing a pattern of poor behavior, you need to be objective about what you are truly valuing in that relationship.

TAKEAWAY

Take a moment to ask yourself, in what circumstances have you tolerated poor behavior from people? Did they have more or less social currency than you? See if you can think of a few examples of where on this graph some relationships in your life would fall.

CHAPTER 6

The History of Social Currency

So where did social currency come from? Is it a newly formed element of a digital world? Did it pop into existence No.

Social currency isn't new.

I hear people blaming technology for the rise in depression, general dissatisfaction, and negative body image. While it's clear to me that technology plays a role in these issues, I believe the true culprit is a deeper issue. Technology offers an overexposure to the ways in which we measure the value of people. The issue is actually how we value people and ourselves. If we fix that, we can be exposed to it all we want because it won't be a negative influence on us anymore.

We currently value people based on their social currency.

This isn't an invention that came from the digitization of culture. It's a dynamic that's been at play since the first strangers met. They sized each other up, considered what the other had to offer, and contemplated if they could get further with them than without them. It was a matter of life or death, eat or be eaten, procreation or extinction. Social currency was based on survival.

Take it a few centuries further. People chose partners and friends in order to maintain power and status. Only people of certain status married each other. The wealthy married to consolidate power. You couldn't escape your social currency or change it. The social currency of beauty was much less valued because you didn't need it to survive.

The survival currencies like power and status were the dominant currencies. Over time, as humanity became wealthier and more civilized, having an attractive or talented partner became more important to some than the consolidation of power. Now, when selecting a mate, we often subconsciously ask ourselves if we will progress socially because of that person, not just survive.

The social currencies evolve to adapt to what society and culture currently values, just like traditional currencies change to adapt to how people spend money (credit cards, Apple Pay, etc.). However, it's important to note that these adaptations are still versions of the original currencies—USD, euro, pound, etc.

Social Currency and Stereotypes: Race, Gender & Sexuality

Humans are hardwired to make snap decisions; it's how we survived this long. We learn things, recognize patterns, and make choices based on those patterns. Right or wrong, we assign social currency to people in an instant. It's a form of privilege that many people are unaware of, but it's real and very impactful to society, for better or worse.

To understand the influence of race, gender, and sexuality on social currency, you first have to understand that social currency is nothing new. It didn't just pop into existence with the invention of Facebook or Instagram, or even the internet in general. No, social currency is something human beings have been trading since the dawn of civilization; it just hasn't had an official name.

There was a time your social currency was directly linked to your chance of survival. Think of the caste system. Only people of certain status could speak to each other, marry each other, or have certain jobs. Going back even further, there were the beautiful women in Sparta taken to be oracles. Social currency has been tied to race and gender for centuries.

But let's focus on the 20th century since it's a little closer to home. Back in the 1950s, women, people of color, and anyone on the LGBTQ+ spectrum carried much less social currency than they do today. (And let's be real—these groups *still* carry less social currency across the board, especially when it comes to the power and status forms of social currency. But I don't think anyone will argue with me when I say that the disparity was even more extreme back then.)

During this period of American history, straight white men had the lion's share of social currency, as they have for pretty much all periods of history. Since social currency is tied to attention, this means their faces were the ones on magazine covers, movie posters, and TV commercials. Their names were the ones on ballot boxes, newspaper bylines, and books. Their voices were the ones on the radio and at university lecterns. No matter which slice of society you look at—whether the movie machine in Hollywood or the political machine in D.C. or anywhere else in between—people gave their attention to straight white men.

Attention is closely tied to trust. Let's say you go to two different doctors, and each one gives you a different opinion on your medical issue. One doctor is a white male, and the other is a woman of color. If you grow up seeing only white men in positions of power and authority, you're more likely to put your trust in the white male doctor—not for any scientifically valid reason, but just because we tend to trust what we're used to. In this way, the spending and receiving of social currency can be a vicious cycle that rewards those who already have it—not unlike how the top 1% of earners in this country make so much money that their passive income is higher than their salaried income. Their money makes money. It's the same with social currency.

While our culture has made important strides toward equality in the decades since the 1950s, there is still an uneven distribution of attention and therefore social currency awarded to some groups over others. The disparity depends on which kind of social currency you're looking at—beauty, power, or status. For instance, Beyoncé—a woman of color—arguably has all three in spades. Her beauty and talent led to her fame, which led to her wealth, which led to her power and status. But if you were to stick Beyoncé in a board room full of Ivy League professors interested in bragging to each other about their latest publications, Beyoncé's clout would only take her so far.

Speaking personally, even though my physical appearance has always afforded me a certain degree of social currency, I discovered pretty quickly upon entering the workforce that when it comes to power and status, men have a leg up in our patriarchal society.

This became obvious to me when I was met with considerably more doubt, disrespect, and threats to "speak with my manager" when I started in my corporate sales role. I learned my strategies from the best sales reps on my team—I was the only woman on the team, so naturally, all my responses were influenced by how I heard the men on my team speak to their clients and prospects.

For the most part, it worked well. Once in a while, I would run across someone who didn't like strength and certainty coming from an email signed with a woman's name.

They told me I was "unprofessional" even when I sent the exact same email one of my male counterparts had no issue sending. Once you get past the frustration and gaslighting, it's actually quite entertaining to watch. The best part is when my manager I send them to is also a woman. Gotcha. Have fun with that one, Chris.

Thankfully, that doesn't happen as often or as blatantly as it used to, but it still happens. The race part of social currency influences beauty and power the most, but status is impacted as well. We assume people have expertise (status) because of how they look. We assume people are talented singers or athletes (beauty) because of how they look. We assume people are in charge, they're the owner of the business, etc. (power) because of how they look.

Our brains like to do this because it's the path of least resistance. Our brains assume things like this the same way they assume chairs are for sitting and broccoli is for eating. That's the context we've seen this object in the most—so it's probably the same in *this* context.

The thing is, people aren't objects. So you have to consciously redirect your brain, training yourself to slow your judgments in regard to how you evaluate people.

Changing Your Social Currency

Historically, there was much less you could do about changing the social currency you had. You were born with a fixed amount of it. If your dad was a farmer, you were also a farmer. If your dad was a king, hey—lucky you, you'd also become king one day. If you were beautiful, great. If not, forget lip fillers and BBLs; you couldn't even get concealer or mascara. Sure, there were ancient beauty treatments—some of them fascinatingly brutal—but those don't compare to the laser facials and implants we have in the 21st century. Or even just slapping on an Instagram filter and calling it a day.

Not to mention the way technology allows us to create "perfect" music and art. Before, you would have to sing the note on key in order to create great music. Now you have autotune and a thousand other programs to tweak your vocals.

While the ability to increase your social currency is definitely on the rise, the currencies themselves evolve and the values fluctuate. For instance, in most circles, being a self-made millionaire is praised more than inheriting wealth. That's because—thanks to our Puritan forefathers—we Americans have a high regard for work ethic, earning your success, and dedication. But that wasn't always the case. People who worked for a living used to be commoners. The feudal system in Europe separated peasants from kings, and to work hard was to be considered less worthy.

The social currency of status is changing as well. It used to be that people with degrees, accreditations, etc., were trusted above anyone else. Now, with the explosion of the information age and the availability to fact check everything, people don't value institutional accreditation as much as they used to.

Work experience can get you a job that a college degree can. With the increase in the number of people getting college degrees, the value of that in the marketplace is decreasing (remember the economics lesson from earlier?). We learn in different ways, and we want to learn from people we like and people who have been in our same situation.

Perhaps the most striking change of all is that today, earning a living for yourself gives a sense of pride and purpose. If you didn't work for what you have, you're viewed as less interesting or less deserving than someone who did. People will value the social currency (and in this case, actual currency) that goes along with being close to someone who comes from generational wealth, but valuing the actual person is less common and more challenging unless they have the life assets and social virtues that make them a good friend.

No one wants a trust fund baby; they just want the trust fund. This is why having high social currency can lead to loneliness. People rarely take the time to get to know you as a person because they're distracted by what they can get from you. On the other hand, people with high social currency aren't always required to be a "good friend" in order to have "friends." The bar is lower for them, sometimes causing a deficit in their social virtues because their social currency carries them in most relationships.

TAKEAWAY

While social currency is not new to this century—at least not in the same way Bitcoin is—the internet and social media make it relevant in new ways by introducing exponentially more things for us to pay attention to. As our values as a society evolve and change, so does the role of social currency.

PART TWO:

Investing Attention

CHAPTER 7

Where Is Your Addiction?

After getting an overview of each type of social currency in Part 1, you probably have an idea of your particular poison—the currency you value most that you're personally motivated to acquire.

For me, it was beauty—I wanted to feel secure in my worth as a woman. I thought the way to get that security was through validation by men. The cultural message we receive as women is, "You are not complete until you have the approval of, and lifelong commitment from, a man." And how do you get that? A smokin' body.

But social currency is addictive. Your tolerance grows. The more attention I got, the more I needed in order to feel validated. It wasn't enough to be attractive; I wanted to be more attractive than other women. It grew into a nasty obsession with being the most attractive woman in the room. I needed to be the one getting the most attention in order to feel secure. If I couldn't compete with another woman's beauty, fine, I'd dig into my social currency purse and add up the ways I could be worth more than her. My inner dialogue went a little something like this:

Okay, she's prettier than you…but I bet you're smarter than her. She probably didn't go to college, and if she did, she certainly didn't major in economics or pay off her student loans in two years. Yeah, she's in good shape, but has she run a marathon? No. She can't compete with you—when you look at the whole picture, you've got her beat.

This ego-soothing form of self-regulating trained me to compare and compete in order to feel confident. It taught me that in order to feel good about myself, I needed to criticize others any time I felt threatened. Where did it come from? How did I learn to do this in order to make myself feel superior? Stories. Movies. Cultural narratives. The idea that you must compete—and win—to be worthy.

No matter which social currency you're investing in, trading in, and measuring your worth in, the result is always the same. At some point, you end up thinking to yourself, *This isn't enough,* And eventually I started wondering, *Is there something wrong with me?*

If I went hours or days without attention and validation, I would doubt my worth in the eyes of others. I would doubt if I really was valuable to anyone. I would question if my boyfriend really loved me. So I went out to find new validation, or more of it. Which is why social media is a dangerous game for those addicted to validation.

Just like with any drug, the more frequently you use it—and the higher intensity these experiences—the more of it you need to feel the effect. If your phone is always blowing up with notifications from thousands of people liking "you," the real person in front of you, spending time and attention with you, might not mean as much, or their attention might not feel as good as it otherwise would.

This might not seem like a dangerous addiction compared to slot machines and cocaine, but think of all the relationships that are hurt or broken because of insecurity, comparison, and competition. An addiction to social currency feeds all of that. It's important to know some groups are more vulnerable to this addiction than others.

Beautiful women are at the highest risk for developing this addiction. Why? You might guess celebrities, models, and the Hollywood types are in the most vulnerable group. But consider this, having high social currency due to fame or extreme success in your given field typically happens gradually. You also realize it comes with the territory. No one pursues a career in acting, makes it big, and is surprised when they're followed by paparazzi. If you want to live a low-key life, maybe don't pursue a career in the spotlight. But for women born into a body that fits the current beauty standard, simply existing attracts attention they didn't ask for.

And what about attractive men? Can't they be at risk for this addiction? Yes, but women are at a higher risk, comparatively, because culture pays attention to the physical appearance of women more than the physical appearance of men. This is why they are at the highest risk for developing this addiction; it happens without them even knowing it.

Whether you're trying to get people to look at you or not, if you're a beautiful woman, you notice people noticing you. At first, you think it's a coincidence, but then you realize you actually have influence over people. You realize you can use your appearance to get what you want. People listen to you, look at you, and generally do what you want them to because they value your social currency of beauty.

For me, I first noticed this influence in high school, when I discovered I could get boys to do things if they wanted to be my boyfriend. This grew into seeing how much attention I could get from how many boys all at once. It turned into a little game. It's not a part of my story I'm proud of, but I'm not too proud to admit it. I knew the influence I had and wondered to what extent I could put it to use. My conscience kicked in pretty quickly, but not before doing quite a bit of damage. No matter how many guys texted me, wanted me, or broke up with their girlfriends for me…it wasn't enough.

Once I "got them," I wanted someone else. Once I lost one, I needed a replacement. I thought maybe it was because I didn't commit and a deeper connection, a long-term relationship, would be different. If I could get a guy to commit to me for life, that would prove I was valuable and significant.

I found myself on a path towards settling down with the wrong guy because I wanted to get married before I was "too old" (whatever that means). Taking steps in a relationship felt like progress (I'm not sure why), and I wanted to make progress in my personal life, not just my professional life.

But as the ring slipped on my left hand, I felt a sinking feeling in my heart. Being engaged didn't solve any problems in the relationship—and it didn't feel like progress. It felt like working all day for someone and getting handed Monopoly money at the end. I felt lost, confused, and lied to.

When you're wealthy, you can choose to show it off. When you're talented, you can choose to share it publicly. But when you're beautiful…your social currency is on your face. It's in your skin. Sometimes you can't hide it even when you try. People comment on your beauty when you're not asking for it. It's hard to avoid the validation sometimes. You need to be conscious of how deeply you let it sink into your self-worth.

There was a period of time I intentionally tried to look bad so people would leave me alone. I needed treatment for this addiction. I went cold turkey and took a "beauty break."

I stopped wearing makeup, stopped shaving, stopped putting any kind of effort into the way I looked. I had to detox and cleanse myself from the habit of boosting my confidence through attention and compliments. This habit formed without my consent. I didn't realize I was only confident so long as I was getting validation from my beauty. This can happen with any of the social currencies.

The investment banker who's only confident so long as he drives the latest Rolls Royce. The model who's only confident so long as she gets hundreds of thousands of "likes" on her Instagram posts. The father who's only confident so long as his children continue to do well in high-school sports.

This detox experiment challenged me to reflect on this pattern. I learned things about myself, not all of them positive. I realized I quickly got attached to anyone who gave me excessive amounts of attention. In the dating world, this made me an easy target for narcissists and possessive men.

This also revealed I didn't have many genuine hobbies—things I did for the sake of doing them. I would work out, but that was to control my body. I would go to parties, but that was to be "seen" at the party. So much of my attention was distracted by maintaining my social currency, I didn't realize I wasn't investing in things I actually valued.

I learned to see myself as more than my body and eventually developed a sense of self-worth that wasn't rooted in social currency, but social virtues.

After the "beauty break," I slowly re-introduced things to my body care routine. Not because I felt like I had to, but because I actually wanted to. I realized I didn't have to reject all forms of beauty because of the unwanted attention. I knew in order to really enjoy who I was, I had to create space for expressing myself. I started practicing.

Before, I'd shave my legs or put on makeup because I felt pressure to meet the cultural expectation that women should be hairless, pore-less, and flawless. Now, when I choose to do anything with my body, it's because I want to. It's for my own enjoyment, self-expression, or opportunity to feel connected with my body. I'm proud to say the relationship I have with my appearance is the healthiest it's ever been—and the addiction is gone. (If you are struggling with your relationship with your body, get resources at *www.thebodyimagesolution.com*).

Beyond just physical appearance, anyone whose social currency is obvious or inherited is at risk for "accidental addictions" like this.

When you aren't actively controlling where you attention goes, new patterns form without your awareness. You do things mindlessly. You react to things wanting your attention instead of responding on your terms. Your phone lights up, and you immediately check it.

Reactionary attention patterns lead to validation addiction. You compulsively check your phone, and if there's no validation waiting, no text, no likes, no email, no messages, you feel sad. Your expectation isn't met. Eventually, you pay attention to anything that will give you a sense of validation, even if it's a cheap version. Anything that flashes before you or lights up your phone is something you chase. You forget to invest in things, people, and ideas with substance. Don't get me wrong, attention has value, but it's shallow and unfulfilling when it's not paired with depth.

But by now, if you're following directions, you're unaware of that email that could've stolen your attention for a few minutes or hours. Now you wait until you're ready to check your messages—you'll see it on your terms. Your attention is within your control. You're not reacting; you're intentionally checking. It hits different.

Action Steps

Now that your social and email notifications are tucked away in their respective apps, it's time to go one level deeper.

1. I want you to turn off text and Messenger notifications. In fact, go ahead and turn off badges for everything except texts and phone calls. This way, your phone isn't constantly lighting up with each bid for your attention.

A Telefonica study estimates the average smartphone user gets as many as 63.5 notifications per day. I dug into this research and found some concerning information. The study was published in 2014, which may as well be a billion years ago in digital time. Their sample size is embarrassingly low (15), and while there are more recent sources, they all point to this one study. What's concerning to me beyond the stale data is that this isn't being studied more.

Let me remind you, we didn't even have Facebook Messenger in 2014. We didn't have Uber. 2014 may as well have been the Stone Age, but it's the most recent data I could find, and it's being referenced in recent articles like it's still relevant. So… fine. Let's say, for the sake of argument, it's 63 notifications. That's 63 times your phone lights up to bid for your attention. That's 63 opportunities for distraction. That's 63 chances for your concentration to break, even if you're already on your phone. That's 63 "transaction costs" of switching your attention from one thing to another.

That's a lot. And we all know it's more than 63.

2. Don't stop with your phone. Take the plunge and turn off desktop notifications for both personal and work computers. That means no work email, no Slack or Teams, nothing unless you choose to click it open and check.

How many work emails do you get per day? How many times does your Slack *ding* or your Teams icon start flashing? Those are distractions. Those are micro doses of validation because it's a chance for someone to be wanting you.

The way to take back control over this addiction is to turn down the frequency. Turn down the intensity. Turn down the access.

Depending on your job, this may or may not be possible. But don't be too quick to jump into the "not possible for me" camp. See what you can do, and do what you can.

3. If having notifications on your phone is a requirement for your job, request a separate work phone and explain this boundary to your employer.

Confining your work messages to a designated device means that when you open your personal phone, the only indications you should see that people are trying to get ahold of you will be a little badge on your SMS text messages, or if you missed a phone call.

That's it. Think about it. When you're reading an article or important email on your phone, you won't be interrupted by the banner notification that someone texted you. You also avoid pretty much all embarrassing notifications, like a Hinge match while you're on a date. Or a text from your ex when you're showing your friend a meme on your phone.

If you don't have notifications, you don't have interruptions.

4. Turn on your read receipts, if you can. It's the courteous thing to do to clue people in on when you've actually seen their messages. Also, if the person is a frequent contact, and you don't have notifications on, they'll know their message hasn't reached you yet. This way, they know they need to call if it's important—when you haven't seen their message. You're

giving them insight on the new way you interact with your phone. Or, if it's a new connection, let them know how you use your phone, and stick to it even if it annoys them or they don't understand.

My number of notifications are next to zero. I get notifications when someone calls me and when my Calm app reminds me to start winding down for sleep at 9:45 p.m. That's it!

TAKEAWAY

I'm a business owner/coach, have a full-time job, host a podcast, have roommates, siblings, parents, friends, and go on dates sometimes. If I can live without notifications, so can you.

The truth is, you don't owe someone immediate access to your attention. That's all a notification is. People survived in a world before instant access, they will survive—and even thrive—without it.

Trust me, there's always an excuse to think you need your source of validation. Take this one step at a time, one category at a time, if necessary. And make sure the people closest to you know how to get your immediate attention if it's urgent.

CHAPTER 8

Identity Beyond Social Wealth

Introductions are awkward for me. I don't know what to say. When I only had a corporate sales job, it was a lot easier, but now that I have multiple forms of income, careers, interests, etc., it just gets messy when people ask, "What do you do?"

People identify strongly with their careers. *I'm a police officer, I'm a lawyer, I'm a singer*, etc., but that's really just what you do for money. That's not who you are. If you think about it, you identify in ways that align with how other people define you.

You might identify as your physical features: "I'm tall," or "I'm brunette."

Some people identify as their flaws: "I'm an overthinker," or "I'm a procrastinator."

While others identify as their relation to other people: "I'm single," or "I'm a mom."

But none of these things truly define who you are as a person. They are facts about your current circumstances, but circumstances, as we both know, change. They can change quickly. Placing your identity in your circumstances increases the risk for an identity crisis. That's why a breakup can feel like the end of your life and losing your job can feel like losing your sense of purpose.

Who you are is deeper than surface-level circumstances. In order to have a solid identity, you need to root yourself in things that either don't change or are within your control. When I was struggling with body image, I thought I *was* the way I looked. This was a result of the constant cultural focus on women's bodies. I internalized this message, and it set mental traps for me constantly. Anytime I wasn't getting attention, I was anxious and uncomfortable. Beautiful women get attention, I thought, *Why am I not getting attention? Does that mean I'm not a beautiful woman? I should've worn a different outfit.*

It went beyond feeling unattractive or undesirable; it was a threat to my very identity. I wasn't really me if I wasn't looking my best.

The way I broke out of that pattern was by finding deeper ways to identify. I had to undo the internalization of the cultural norm to see beautiful women as sexualized bodies first, and people second (or maybe third, let's be honest).

But it's not only the social currency of beauty that culture uses to define your identity.

Culture will identify you as the amount of beauty, status, or power you have, in different forms. You're not a person, you're a number in a bank account, a blue checkmark on Instagram, or a college degree.

You can't control how culture identifies you, but you can control how you identify yourself. When you fall into the pattern of getting your identity from social currency, you also measure your self-worth in terms of social currency. That's why you feel embarrassed if you don't have as many followers, you delete a post if it doesn't get enough "likes," and you compare yourself to people getting high amounts of attention—even if you don't like what they're getting attention for. Or maybe you're getting a high amount of attention because of your social currency and you anchor your value in that. You feel good because you get tens of thousands of "likes" every time you post. You feel validated when you look at your bank account. You feel safe when you have people wanting you. Even when you have high social currency, it becomes dangerous to put your self-worth in these things.

Because when any of these are challenged or begin to evolve, it results in more than just a change in your life; it's a full-blown identity crisis.

Rather than identifying as your social currencies, which need social validation to have value, you can have confidence in your self-worth by identifying as things that don't change. When you change how you identify, you will change how you measure your worth.

You can place your identity in things that aren't relative, things that aren't dependent on other people agreeing. Not everyone agrees on the value of your social currency; what one person values, another rolls their eyes at. This leads you to constantly feeling like you aren't enough, or that you always need to double check to confirm people still value the currency you carry.

Here's the thing. You, as a human, have intrinsic value. The chances of you coming into the world are so small, there has to be a purpose for it. Whether or not you believe in God, by the sheer statistics alone, you have to admit there's something intriguing about the creation of life.

You were born with talents and a purpose. Those talents are different from what other people were born with. So there must be some reason you have them. It's your job to explore them, expand them, and refine them. You don't need to change them, you don't need to validate them, and you don't need to ignore them. But doing those last few things gives you a sense of control over your worth. When you try to change your talent, you feel in control. When your talent is validated, it gives you a sense of control. Even ignoring and wasting your talent gives you a sense of control. If you never pursue your potential, you'll never realize the limits of your talent. Wasted talent is one of the ultimate signs of insecurity. It brings you a false sense of control when you reject something before it rejects you.

Why do we try to control, validate, or even ignore our talent? Because it's uncomfortable to believe the alternative; that your worth doesn't change based on your performance. It's hard to trust that your worth is constant. For some reason, it feels safer for you to have to earn it, measure it, and control it.

If you want to be a good steward of your talent, you should do something with it, not squander it out of fear of disapproval. The intent behind growing your talent should be to express who you are instead of to get attention or approval from people.

Forming Your Identity Based on Your Likes and Interests

The danger of using social currency as the measure for which you gauge your interest in a topic or person is that you're letting popularity guide your interest. You like what everyone else likes. You pay attention to what's trending. It's fast fashion over iconic looks.

Both can get you attention, but one is fleeting while the other is foundational. You have to continually chase one, while the other is consistent. Substance doesn't have to show off, but it's easy to get lost in a flashy world filled with social currency.

Flash is really nice, though, isn't it? Flash is fun. Flash is exciting. But flash is exactly that—here one moment and gone the next. Without pursuing things with substance, there's no chance for our attention to be invested in something meaningful.

We are easily impressed by things that don't actually have meaning— number of followers, views, etc.—but that doesn't mean the account is worth paying attention to. When you look at the content on the page, the quality of the show you're binge watching, is it really something you like? Is it something you're interested in? Or is it something everyone else likes, so you feel obligated to participate?

Maybe you go the other way and reject things that are mainstream. You see yourself as "above" mainstream media and force yourself to like weird stuff just because no one else likes it and it makes you feel superior. Um. Barf. Seriously, gag me. Reminds me of my narcissistic ex-boyfriend who shamed me for liking Maroon 5 better than his favorite German rap group.

Same illness, different symptoms. Rejecting something only because you feel pressure to like it is still rooted in insecurity. It's two sides of the same coin, my guy. What's wrong with liking things you like? No matter if it's mainstream or niche? The only thing that matters is if you *actually* like it. And no one can determine that except you.

Like the things you actually like.

If no one else was around, what would you truly like? What would you watch? What would you listen to? What would make you laugh?

Those are things with true intrinsic value. Things that are good because you like them, not because you think they will give you social currency by liking (or rejecting) them. It's like when I used to pretend I liked sports so guys would think I'm cool. Then I'd be annoyed that all my boyfriend wanted to do was watch football and hockey. Whose fault was that? Mine. My fault. Because I lied. I don't like them. Sometimes I'll enjoy going to a baseball game or watching the finals of something. But I will walk away from conversations about sports. I can't think of a worse way to spend time. But that's just me. And that's okay. I had to stop thinking I needed to adjust who I was to attract someone.

Partner Selection as an Identity Component

While we're at it, let's talk about partners. Social currency plays a huge role in partner selection, whether you want to admit it or not. Take a look and see if any of this hits.

Let's say there's a single guy in L.A. He's done well for himself, he's in his mid-forties, and he's looking for someone to spend time with.

The smart, independent girl who won the affection of his finicky cat is a going to be a more substantive partner than the one with 400,000 followers on her thirst-trap Instagram.

But who does he chase? The popular girl. Because people pay more attention to her, he thinks she's the best prize. Her social currency is clouding his judgment. When he gets her, he thinks she will add to his power and status. People see someone with her influence choose him, and now figure he must also be important. That's how social currency transactions work. She validates his ego and increases his social currency; he does the same for her. Then they both realize there's nothing deeper to their connection than increasing their social currency.

What happens when he actually catches her? He's stuck with a person addicted to a high daily dose of validation. Someone who cares about getting the right photo, not about actually having a good time. Someone who, deep down, he knows will leave him for a guy with more money, more fame, more social currency.

Part of him feels good because when thousands of people like her posts, he gets to be the one she goes home with. He's benefiting from her social currency. But he can't stand to be in the room with her. Plus, she doesn't really look like her pictures. What he's getting isn't actually real. It's an illusion.

He pulls up the Instagram of the smart, independent girl who didn't spend a minute chasing after him. A few posts, a few hundred followers, literally doesn't care what people think of her because she's enjoying herself. And he's left wondering where he went wrong, when the answer is so obvious even his cat knew from the beginning.

How did the cat know? Cats don't deal in social currency. Animals are a great judge of character because they don't know who's hot and who's not. They don't know your Instagram. They can't see your bank account or smell if your perfume is Chanel or Bath & Body Works.

All they can sense is your presence. Your spirit. Your genuine happiness. But that's easy to lose sight of when you start trading in social currency. It's so appealing, such a quick fix for insecurity, we pursue that instead of meaningful relationships. It doesn't stop with relationships, though.

Popularity Versus Intrinsic Value

When you look at the account of an influencer with millions of followers, do you initially feel impressed because of their vanity metrics? Yes. That's human nature, but you need to go deeper and find if there's intrinsic value for you. If there is, okay, great. If there isn't, you have to be able to self-regulate your feelings and thoughts about what impresses you.

Separate your assumptions from what's actually taking place. You can assume something is good because it's popular, but is that always true? I think of the McDonald's hamburger. That's the most popular burger in the world, but is it the best? Absolutely not.

This approach of taking a minute to find intrinsic value helps you avoid the pitfall of judging people (and yourself) only by their social currency.

Social currency "blinds" people who don't separate this snap-judgment instinct. It's why beautiful women have to work extra hard to be taken seriously in professional fields. During my time in corporate sales, I overheard several conversations my colleagues had about women in the office who "we all know why she got promoted," followed by laughter and glances over shoulders to see if I heard them. I did. Even if it wasn't directed specifically at me, I knew that was an indication of conversations about me they wouldn't dare have while I was within earshot.

It might be a popular belief that men favor attractive women, but is it possible she earned it? It might be common for a team member with higher status to give the best advice, but is that true in every case? Don't let popular assumptions based on social currency cloud your vision.

Another path you could be walking down is the need to prove yourself through accreditations and institutions. Needing to pass a strict, rigorous test to show how worthy and capable you are. You might be a lawyer or doctor. You may have gone to a bougie Ivy League college. You care about things like credentials, societies, and associations. This is a sign the social currency of

status is very important to you. You pursue institutional validation for the sake of popularity, not the intrinsic learning process.

The institution of marriage is popular to validate a commitment
you have to someone. To validate you as an adult. But even
marriage, prestigious awards, and elite associations leave you
feeling empty if you pursue them only for popularity.

This is the insurmountable height of climbing the social currency
popularity ladder. Eventually, you either get to the end of your
life with regrets, or you realize you must change the things you're
paying attention to and using to value yourself.

I reached a point where if my patterns were to continue, in any
one of these three social currency directions, I would be building
my identity and confidence based on temporary popularity, not
my values. That's a high-risk investment, with very little reward.
Luckily, I caught this pattern early, but it's never too late.

Exercise: Finding Self-Worth

If the addiction to social currency and external validation comes
from a lack of self-worth, the answer isn't more social currency;
it's more self-worth. How do you do that? Well, we value everything based on what its purpose is. You value the quality of a
school bus based on its ability to transport a large number of
people. You value the quality of a racecar based on speed. You
value the quality of a commuter car based on gas mileage. Each
one is a vehicle, but they're measured based on the purpose,
which is informed by their identity.

The same is true for your personal self-worth. In order to value yourself in the right way, you need to figure out your identity. Are you a race car, commuter car, or a school bus? Obviously, you're none of these things, but you get the idea. How you identify influences how you value yourself.

I'd like you to put down this book for a second and go find a pencil and paper. (Yes, for real! Don't use your phone.) Once you have a pencil and paper, I want you to write down a few identifiers you hold. When you think of who you are, what are a few words that come to mind? How are you currently identifying?

Here's a common sample list from a client I worked with a few years ago:

I'm married
I'm a nurse
I'm 5'6"
I'm blonde
I'm thin
I'm beautiful
I'm funny
I'm a mom
I'm thoughtful

Notice how many of these identifiers can change in an instant. If someone criticizes her appearance, she might not feel beautiful. She could get divorced, or her spouse could pass away. Same with her children. She could lose her hair.

Look at the things she's holding onto that give her value and an identity:

Spouse, children, appearance, career.

The only two things on her list that aren't external are her sense of humor and thoughtfulness. Those are the traits I told her to expand on. After working together, we made a new list. We found new things to attach her identity and value to so she's not addicted to getting validated for subjective things that can change. Here's the new list:

I'm thoughtful
I'm patient
I'm honest
I'm dedicated
I'm loyal
I'm trustworthy
I'm active
I'm expressive
I'm magnetic
I'm caring

All these things roll up into the external qualities listed above, but these are depth-of-character traits that can remain true regardless of whether they are validated by social currency. She could get divorced, change career paths, dye her hair, and still identify as all these things.

Each of these qualities has value in and of itself. Being loyal has value outside of a marriage. Being dedicated has value outside of a career. Being expressive has value outside of beauty.

TAKEAWAY

Shift your current identifiers away from physical traits, career choices, or relationship status and define yourself based on character traits that remain constant regardless of your social or physical circumstances.

CHAPTER 9

Sink, Swim, or Surf

By now, social currency might feel like looking up at a big wave about to crash over you. It has so much momentum, you fear you have no choice but allow it to carry you with its current. But it's just water. It's just waves. Remember, when the waves come, you can either sink, swim, or smile because you learned how to surf.

Powerful forces can be harnessed for your benefit. You just have to understand them first.

Sinking in social currency is allowing it to consume you. When you allow your current social currency to continue defining your self-worth and how you value other people, you're giving into its power. You release all accountability and surrender to whichever direction the waves toss you. In practical terms, you feel empty. Hopeless. Lacking in motivation.

Swimming, on the other hand, means trying to fight back. When you try to keep up with the things society values, increase your social currency, you gain traction at first but tire yourself out quickly. You don't have energy left for enjoying yourself. At the end of the day, you fought hard with nothing meaningful to show for it. This means you feel lonely. Isolated. Exhausted from all the effort.

Surfing in social currency—the most desirable of the three outcomes— is only possible after learning enough about the wave to properly equip yourself and use its momentum for your benefit. Is it dangerous? Yes. But the way I see it is, you're in this ocean either way—so you may as well have some fun. When you master the art of surfing in social currency, you expect to rise, fall, and respond to the different waves as they come. You feel exhilarated. Adventurous. Brimming with confidence.

By now you've learned enough about social currency to see that it is powerful, attractive, and even addictive. Next, you'll learn a few ways to start taking back control over how it influences you. You're already off to a great start with the small action steps we covered in the last few chapters, but adjusting your phone and social media notifications can only get you so far. Before you can go from mindless spending of social currency to strategic investing—in other words, before you can surf—you have to learn to carefully budget your attention. It all starts with accountability.

Taking Accountability for Your Attention

Accountability is a wonderful thing. It's the only way to feel in control of your life. Determining how you contribute to a problem, while uncomfortable, reminds you where you have control over fixing it. If a circuit keeps breaking because I'm vacuuming while watching TV, I can take accountability for that, turn the TV off, and avoid the problem. It doesn't do any good to blame the circuit, continue vacuuming, and be frustrated or surprised every time it breaks. If you're part of the problem, you can be an effective part of the solution.

Humans have a tendency to believe they, as individuals, don't contribute to cultural problems. No one sees themselves as the villain in the story. We don't want to believe we contribute to problems, but the truth is we all do at different points in time, in different intensities.

So, as you continue to read this book, keep in mind you are part of this problem. So am I, by the way. We all are. Being aware of a problem isn't enough to solve it, either. You can *know* the circuit is going to break a few minutes into vacuuming, but if you don't take accountability to fix it, it will keep happening. Which is why it's important we all take accountability for the pieces we contribute to the social currency problem. Realizing harmful patterns, identifying your role in them, and taking bold action to change what you can control is a powerful approach to problem solving and improving your life.

But before you can take accountability and start investing attention in things you truly value, you first have to admit there's a problem with how you're spending your time and attention.

Think about the last time you felt stressed or anxious. What were you trying to do? Nine out of ten times, you were attempting to control something not within your control. You tried producing an outcome rather than being intentional about your actions. That's a natural tendency I fall into as well, but when you try to hold yourself accountable for what's outside your control, you invite stress, anxiety, and depression into your life. And let's be honest—no one wants that.

You are accountable only for the things you can control. When you feel powerless against something, take stock of the things you can control—and surrender to the rest.

Detoxing Your Digital Space

Let me say something that should be obvious but apparently isn't to a lot of people: You don't owe anyone your attention.

Your digital following, friend list, email subscriptions, etc., is within your control. There's no shame in removing influences from your life if they're disrupting your peace. You don't have to be Facebook friends with your hometown crush to see if they're still married and miserable. You don't have to subscribe to the newsletter about politicly charged topics that give you anxiety. You don't have to follow the Instagram fitness accounts that promise "6-pack abs in 6 weeks" and make you feel guilty for ordering truffle fries instead of cauliflower.

Bottom line: You don't have to interact with any content you don't want to see. In fact, the more you comment on or "react" to the content that makes you angry or upset, the more of it you will see in your feed. So if social media stresses you out because all you see is things you don't like, that's an indication of how you're using the platform. Stop looking at things you don't want to give attention to.

When I felt stressed out by my phone, I knew it was time to make a change. Every app sucked the energy and attention out of me. I couldn't focus on what I actually wanted to do. It was time to purge.

So, in 2020, I unfollowed hundreds of Instagram accounts. I unfriended hundreds of people on Facebook. I disconnected from hundreds of people on LinkedIn. I unsubscribed from dozens of email lists.

And no, you don't have to do the weird announcement of, "If you're seeing this post, you made the cut. I just purged my friend list, blah blah blah…"

Don't be that guy. Go about your business for your own sake, not for—you know—attention.

You don't have to go off the deep end and delete *all* your social media accounts. That's a bit extreme. That's like throwing away every bottle of wine in the house and joining AA because you got too drunk once. Try a little moderation first; see how it feels. Digital platforms have the potential to add healthy, unique, interesting things to your life.

Remember that when you like or comment, or even watch something for a long time…the algorithm knows. Whatever you're paying attention to, the algorithm is going to show you more of that. So you actually have more control than you think. You have complete control over what you see, really. So be intentional about it.

> Change your relationship with digital platforms, and you'll change your life.

These digital platforms are powerful tools to share ideas, connect with interesting people, learn, get inspired, laugh, etc., but you're using them wrong if you're stressed out by them. That's not a judgment; it's an observation. One that I had of myself not too long ago.

Since I implemented all the action steps in this first section, the days seem longer. I have more energy. I can freely invest my full attention in people, hobbies, and work. I'm more effective with my time because I'm focused. When you start budgeting your attention, you realize just how much you used to lose during the day.

Am I implying you must always be efficient and effective? Am I about to climb onto a "hustle" your way to happiness soap box? Absolutely not. When you realize the energy and attention you get back, you can invest that into a concept that eludes most of us caught up in the digital world. It's a little thing called rest. I'll cover that in more detail in the next section: Solutions to Budgeting Your Attention.

Learning to Surf

Before going further, let me say you are not unlovable because you make mistakes. You are not unlovable even if you intentionally do selfish things. You are not unlovable because you've harshly judged people (or yourself) based on what's in their social wallet. Before the end of this book, and maybe even so far, if you're being honest, you'll discover some pretty embarrassing things about how you judge people.

You're gonna feel like a bad person. You might feel like you've been a jerk to yourself, to your sister, and definitely to the people you went to high school with. You'll feel bad about how you treated people you dated or never even gave a chance. You'll realize that when you thought you were on an amazing run, a huge tidal wave was actually coming up from behind just waiting to wipe you out. That's normal. It's part of the process of learning to surf.

TAKEAWAY

I promise you that if you're patient with yourself and put in the effort—if you take accountability and detox your digital life—you can harness that powerful tidal wave of social currency for your benefit.

CHAPTER 10

Spending Attention with Intention

Be honest—you judged me. Before deciding to read this book, you ran down a list in your mind of reasons you should care. These reasons could be based on what I look like, my Instagram account/following, or my credentials. Maybe you're a dedicated *Confidently She* listener and know more about my story, but chances are you judged me based on my social currency—and decided, yes.

And you're 100% justified in doing that because it's how everyone is taught to judge people. We are forced to make hundreds of decisions every day. It's hard to think deeply about and accurately judge each one. So instead, you do a quick Google search, maybe look someone up on Instagram, and make your decision.

You do this, so you expect people to do this to you, right? Whether you're aware of it or not, it's happening. Subconsciously, you want to present yourself in the most credible, most attractive, most desirable way so that when someone looks at you, Googles you, or makes that snap judgment about whether or not they should give attention to you, the answer is yes.

This leads to the attention-budgeting issues covered so far. Because you give attention to the things that appear most attractive. You listen to people who have the largest following. You give energy and attention to things that are popular instead of things you value. Why? Because you haven't done the work to explore what it is you actually value. Either that, or you get caught up in what other people are talking about, looking at, and watching—you forget the things that light you up.

Check Your Intentions

"But Rebekah, I really do enjoy looking good," said the woman sitting in front of me. "What am I supposed to do, stop wearing makeup? Stop being hot? Stop dressing nice?"

This is a common line of questions I get after working through insecurities with gorgeous women. Megan was afraid of a few things. The first was being judged only by her social currency. If she continued to present herself in the way she felt most comfortable, people would only see her as an attractive woman with high beauty currency, and nothing more. She would continue to be doubted when she spoke up in a meeting at work, the underlying assumption in the room being that she only got the job because the hiring manager had a crush.

She was also afraid the men she dated wouldn't see her as anything more than a pretty face. Her exes didn't take her seriously and talked down to her when she shared an opinion. She feared that a woman who's beautiful, ambitious, talented, and kind would be too intimidating—so they'd keep her one dimensional in their mind. They'd fall head over heels for how she looks in a dress but ghost her after hooking up.

"You have to do it for yourself," I told her. "You have to look good for yourself, but you also have to know that when you display social currency like that, you're going to attract all kinds of people."

This is why we have terms like "gold digger," "Jersey chaser," "arm candy," "sugar daddy," etc. These are people who want social currency and nothing more. I tell clients, you can go out looking like a 10/10, dressed to the nines, completely at peace with who you are because it's genuine self-expression with zero expectation. Or you can go out looking like a 10/10, dressed to the nines, completely crippled by self-consciousness because it's an attempt to validate yourself using social currency. Exact same action, different vibe.

It's all about *why* you do what you do.

Your intention behind doing or having things is more important than the things you have. Put another way, why you do something is 100% more important than what you do. Roll with me for a second. We're going to sample from my philosophy background for a paragraph or two.

Is ending someone's life wrong? You might say yes. This is a question of ethics and morality, so think carefully. Notice, I didn't say "killing someone," because that phrasing carries certain implications. But the question of ending a life, is that wrong? Always?

I would say, it depends. This is a breeding ground for good debate, but that's not my purpose for bringing it up now. Most countries, civilizations, and governing bodies have laws to permit ending someone's life in specific contexts. If someone is trying to kill you, you can kill them. Self-defense. If someone is suffering from an illness and they will die eventually, you can kill them. (It's called euthanasia—a mercy kill.) So, even within the most extreme example of ending someone's life, the reason you do it matters.

If that's true for something big, it must also be true for everything that falls underneath.

You can have power, beauty, status, and all the forms of social currency in this book, but without the right intentions underlying your actions, you can still find emptiness at the end of the day.

You can have little to no social currency but live with an attitude of thankfulness, generosity, and humility. How? By building the life assets you truly care about. Creating things for the sake of them existing, not for the approval of others. That's where the emptiness comes from, attempting to impress people with your life instead of creating a life that's fulfilling.

Avoid Extremes

Working in personal development, edging on health and wellness, I come across a lot of extreme ideas and radical solutions to humanity's oldest problems. Nowhere is this more true than the problem of weight loss. It seems like every few years some new doctor or health guru comes out with another specialized diet that promises to be the secret to shedding extra pounds once and for all. Whether it's the Keto diet, the Mediterranean diet, or the well-publicized don't-eat-anything-after-8-pm diet, people seem willing to try anything—the more extreme the diet, the better. This is because our brains operate best when presented with extremes. We like black and white. Right and wrong. "Tell me what to do, and I'll do it!"

Extremes aren't sustainable, though. And if it's not sustainable, it's not a solution.

Coming to social currency with this same perspective creates extreme opinions—either extreme rejection of the currency or extreme acceptance. At this point in the book, you might be thinking, *Social currency is bad. I must cut myself off from all forms of social currency I might have if I ever want to be seen as more than that.* Or you might be thinking, *Social currency is good. I must accumulate as many forms as possible so I can have influence in every social setting!*

Or you could take an individual currency approach and see an extreme on either side.

Beauty

"Looks don't matter!" Or, "Looks are all that matter."

Status

"The college you went to doesn't matter!" Or, "The college you went to is all that matters."

Power

"Money doesn't matter!" Or, "Money is all that matters."

The truth is, every single one of those things matter. They just don't matter in every context equally, or to everyone equally.

That's the aim of this book. To unpack in which contexts each of these things "matter." When they matter, they carry influence over others, and even over you.

I'm here to say that beauty matters, and it matters a lot. Power matters, and it matters a lot. Status matters, and it matters a lot.

But it doesn't matter the same to everyone, and it won't carry its value the same over time.

With each of these currencies, ask yourself:

- "What am I currently doing with the hope of getting more of this?"
- "Who am I hoping to impress when this project is completed?"
- "Why do I feel like I have to follow through on something I no longer enjoy doing?"

Part of the pursuit of social currency is a fear of failure. You see each setback as a debit to your social currency account. Just like failing a test in school brings your grade down for that class, failing in an attempt to gain social currency brings your balance down.

This may be an unavoidable truth, but the good news is that when you stop seeing social currency as the game, you stop associating your self-worth with that account balance. It's perfectly fine to change your mind. It's okay to "give up" and redirect.

Change Your Mind

One of my proudest moments came from, what some people would call, giving up.

It was December 9, 2018. I texted my fiancé, letting him know I no longer cared when he was coming home from his fourth consecutive weekend hunting trip because I wasn't going to be there.

The relationship hadn't been working for well over a year. The complete lack of respect, regard for my feelings, and emotional support reached a breaking point when he wasn't willing to compromise on going hunting every single weekend (including my birthday) for an entire month, something he neglected to talk with me about before committing to going. You can only have the same conversation so many times before you go from feeling like a crazy person to acting like one—and I wasn't going to go there again.

What swirled in my mind was fear of looking like a failure. Fear that I had wasted years of my life investing in a relationship that ended up, well, ending. My logical side met that fear with some cold reality. First, that the relationship was already a failure. Second, staying inside something that's broken was never going to replace time I spent trying to fix it. In fact, every minute I spent inside the failure of a relationship was another minute wasted. That was time I couldn't spend moving on from it and finding something worth investing in. When the ship is going down, you don't dwell on how long you've been on the ship. You get off.

Also, let's talk about failure for a second. Since when is ending a relationship failing? I've seen plenty of persisting relationships that are complete failures. Yet every anniversary they're celebrated like longevity is the main criteria we use to measure the success of a relationship. I'm not impressed by people who are miserable together year after year. I'm impressed by people who know when it's time to leave a bad situation.

So I knew, for myself, ending this relationship was a win. A triumph in the story of my life. The time where the reader will audibly yell, "YES! Finally!"

But no matter how right I knew the decision was, I was still afraid of looking like a failure. Looking like a failure to whom? My parents? Probably not. Both my sisters are divorced, and I bet they would see me calling off an engagement as divine discernment rather than a failure. So, who, then? His family? Maybe. They didn't like me from the beginning, and they would see this as proof they were right about me. But were they? Yeah, they didn't want me marrying him, but they weren't right about ME. I was leaving because I deserved better, not because he did. I had to realize that my carefully crafted image was not something worth preserving at the expense of my self-respect. I was not going to sacrifice a lifetime of peace for the mere appearance of success.

This isn't just true in relationships. I quit a few times in my career, too. I wanted to focus my professional efforts into something meaningful to me.

My parents did an incredible job of not putting any kind of pressure on me to become like them. They encouraged me to try things. They taught me it's okay to change my mind. This is a recurring theme you'll notice, and a primary reason I learned so much in so few years.

So, I want you to give yourself permission to change your mind. Give yourself permission to quit. Give yourself permission to question the pressure you feel to have your life look a certain way.

I think quitting is awesome when you do it for the right reasons. I think being fired is awesome when it's for the right reasons. In fact, if you haven't been fired—you might need to start being more bold in communicating your ideas. Your ideas are good. People with good ideas get fired sometimes, too. Because someone is either threatened by them or doesn't understand.

Either way, you're better off knowing where your good ideas will be appreciated. I say, speak up and trust you'll recover from the consequences. My parents encouraged that trait in me as well. Standing up for what's right, speaking your mind, but also having social awareness and empathy for others (that took longer for me to learn, but that comes later).

I'm fully aware your parents might be different. They might have ideas of who they want you to be. Those ideas might be communicated passively, actively, or even aggressively. Any pressure from a parent to forge their child's life path for them comes from their own insecurities and the value they place on each social currency.

And it works both ways: There's the dad who wants his son to grow up to be an NFL player because he never got picked for the team, and there's the dad who criticizes his son's ambition to be an NFL player because he never got picked for the team.

Both dads want the best for their sons, but both are letting fear dominate: Fear their sons will get what they want. Fear their sons won't get what they want. Fear their sons will get what they want and have it taken away.

We've all seen the classic pageant mom living vicariously through her six year old, but it commonly happens in less obvious ways. You say things, do things, and decide things with a subconscious influence from the people who raised you. It's how eating disorders start. It's how resentment builds. It's how your cousin spent 12 years going to medical school and is chronically depressed even though his parents are so proud.

> No matter what your situation is, you are allowed to quit. There's nothing "magic" about any given life path. Plenty of doctors are miserable. Plenty of mothers are miserable. Plenty of movie stars are miserable. There's no path that never leads to misery. There's no guaranteed path to happiness.

Here's the thing, you must be okay with people not understanding your decisions. People will misinterpret your actions. Give up anyway. What's there to be afraid of, exactly? Looking dumb? Well, we found the problem. You shouldn't live your life in an effort to avoid looking dumb.

That leads to more unhappiness than failure does. How do you get over that very real fear of looking dumb? The reason you do something must be stronger than the outcome you desire. Because the outcome might be failure. You must be willing to give up on things (and start things) if you want a life of peace, fulfillment, and joy.

Most relationships end. Most businesses fail. Most first attempts are terrible. I can hear you thinking, *Yeah, but I'm different.* I'm sure you are different. You wouldn't be frustrated that success isn't making you happy if you didn't have special talent.

But don't buy into the story that you have to "break the mold" to be a success. Success itself isn't objective. How I define success is different than how you define success. You need to figure out what success would look like for you and why. The why is the important part. Because if the reason you want your success is "to prove everyone wrong," you're not *really* doing it for yourself. So, why do it?

Let's say you're pursuing acting, and your definition of success looks like winning an Oscar. Straight up, you want an Academy Award.

Okay, why? Your first answer could be, "So I would know that I'm the best. To prove to everyone I'm good and I made something of myself."

Alright, let's break that down. Is it true that people who win Oscars are the best? It is true they're good? Because sometimes people win Oscars and they are NOT the best. It took Leonardo DiCaprio forever to win his, and it wasn't even for his best performance. The dude deserved one from the jump, but no, he had to be torn apart by a bear for the Academy to finally hand it over. Do you think anyone was sitting there thinking, *Leo hasn't made something of himself until he wins the Oscar...*

Ahh, of course not. Because the work speaks for itself. You don't need the awards when the work stands on its own. You might get the awards for work like that, but you don't *need* the awards when the work is that good. Awards are subjective. They aren't an absolute measure of what's good and what's bad.

At the end of the day, it's people choosing the winner. There are people who think Leo is trash (those people are wrong, but they exist) no matter how many awards he gets.

On the flip side, you may want to win an Oscar for a different reason. Your answer could be, "To have a tangible goal to work towards."

Okay, there you go. That's totally fine. You're holding it loosely, and the focus can be on the work, not the result. You're not hanging your entire identity and career on one single outcome. Your chances of having a mental breakdown are slim. You take the same steps, stay true to the work (not pandering to what you think will do well), and you won't rake yourself over the coals if you don't get nominated.

The reason why you set a goal matters because it influences the experience you have while working towards the goal. It removes the pressure and helps you focus on the process. So, when you relate this to social currency, the reason you have that currency matters more than the currency itself. You could have the social currency of beauty as a result of being in good physical health, or you could have it as a result of sacrificing your health in an attempt to fit a cultural beauty standard. The former is a sustainable way to have social currency. The latter leads to burnout and insecurity because you're using your body as a means to an end, rather than the end itself.

Investing in Intention

The intent you have while giving attention, energy, and time to something matters. You can invest time in your body directly, without the intent to convert it into social currency to be used for a transaction.

Investing in your body with the intent to use it in a social transaction has a different ROI expectation than investing in your body with the intent to honor and care for yourself.

That was a lot. Here's an example.

You can shower, style your hair, and wear a bold outfit before going to dinner. That alone is not an investment of attention, time, and energy into social currency. It only becomes that when you give it the intention of influencing other people.

If you're doing it because you enjoy being clean, having styled hair, and wearing bold outfits, you've already achieved your desired ROI at that time because you don't have the intention of influencing anyone.

You may end up getting compliments and attention, maybe even a free drink without trying—a passive form of social currency—but passive transactions do not require attention or energy. So, they're free.

Think of passive social currency transactions as dividends paid on an asset. Your body is an asset. Your mind is an asset. Your heart is an asset.

When you invest intentionally in those things, you're creating an appreciating asset that pays social dividends. Not always, but depending on what the stock price is within your given social context, the dividends can be high or low.

The point being, you invested in an asset rather than a currency. You're not expecting to trade or use it, and because of that any influence you have is a bonus because you already own the asset. That asset is worth something. And you're receiving passive influence because of it.

Which is why when you crack the code to social currency, you end up feeling like you have enormous amounts of influence and social value because you're not paying attention to it, but you're getting attention anyway. Your intention with your attention makes all the difference in how it feels accumulating, spending, and investing social currency.

By now we know social currency isn't the right way to value ourselves or other people. What we don't know is what we can really do about it. It's second nature, it's happening all around us, so how do we stop? Everyone wants to be confident and have a high sense of self-worth, but somehow we can't get a grip on it to last us longer than the initial rush of good news.

Anyone can be confident when things are going well. What I'm offering is a way to have a consistent baseline of confidence and self-worth that survives the times things go wrong, when you don't get your way, when someone else wins. Basically, it doesn't disappear when things get difficult.

On the surface, a simple fix would be to create a consistent stream of validation with your currency of choice. Maybe you even mix it up a little. Some days you gain the approval of others with your appearance. When that starts feeling dull, you break down and get that Porche you've had your eye on for years. When that thrill fades, you turn to your career and bank account to give you the boost of assurance you need that you're doing okay. But the pattern repeats again, you start feeling dissatisfied with your work, and now want a raise. But I want you to think back to the last time you had a pay increase and how long it took for that satisfaction to wear off. This is the danger of looking to social currency to fill your need for approval. You can't expect more of the thing that made you sick to cure you.

Plato observed that man is a social and political animal. We have a desire to be accepted by others because the social unit keeps us safe, we have connection, and feel significant. This is not a destructive desire. But when you place the power to measure your worth in the hands of other people, your security goes along with it. When that happens, you find yourself doing all kinds of things to be accepted instead of being who you are and attracting the right people into your life. It seems we never graduate from the school yard where we want to be accepted by the "in crowd."

We also like to see how well we're doing compared to others. We value others based on the same things we use to value ourselves. You're impressed (or threatened) when people have things you lack. You see people as more or less valuable based on the way they stack up against the social currencies you value. Financial currencies are set by governments and accepted within economies to standardize how goods and services are valued and traded.

But this currency, social currency, is more dangerous. We measure the value of people. It's determined by culture and accepted within social circles to standardize how people are valued. We rank people's appearance on scales of 1-10. We judge people's success based on the kind of car they drive. We value people's intelligence based on the university they attended. If you're lacking in one currency, you can make up for it in another to balance and justify your worth.

But why is this dangerous? Human beings have intrinsic value no matter how much social currency they carry. When you commoditize people, you dehumanize them. You treat some people well, and others you easily cast aside. Because you see people as a vehicle to serve your own interests, rather than human beings with feelings, beliefs, and stories of their own.

How do we change it? That's the exciting part. Luckily, this is one of the things within your control.

Our exposure to social currency has increased and intensified with the globalization of culture. With that globalization, the individual has more collective power than ever before. We can mobilize. While culture used to be top-down, determined by big business and marketing campaigns, social currency allows individuals to have influence on what's actually valued.

The popular vote is becoming more meaningful. Which means individual choices matter more now than in the past. Fifty years ago, you could write something on a sign, stand in Times Square, and have a few hundred people pay attention to it. Now, you can protest something on Instagram and have thousands (if not millions) of people see it. Or you can do both, like one of my favorite Instagram accounts. Follow @dudewithsign.

Your reach is crazy, even if it's "only" a few hundred people. When you take control of your attention, time, and energy, you can focus on using your platform to share what truly matters to you. You will need to sacrifice short-term social currency when you make this choice, but in the long run, if you broadcast messages or content you truly believe in, you will build something you're proud of.

The good news about all this is that we have the power to choose what we value. You can invest in the currencies of your choice and, at the end of the day, enjoy what you have without tying your entire identity to it.

We saw this in early 2021 with the GameStop stock surge. Hedge funds placed a bet that the price of GameStop stock would go down. A group of gamers on Reddit caught wind of the bet and decided to troll them. Hard. This was born out of a unique combination of nostalgia towards GameStop and the frustration with establishments that make money no matter which direction the market goes. They invested in GameStop stock even though it wasn't technically worth as much as they were paying for it.

The stock price went through the roof, and the hedge funds lost. In that scenario, everyone knew the business itself was not valued at the price the stock was trading for, but they decided it was worth it to invest anyway. This group of a few thousand people decided collectively that it was worth it, and the price of the stock reflected that. It had very real consequences on these hedge funds when they had to sell their option and lose billions. Some folded entirely.

The economics nerd in me was loving every second of it. The philosophy dork in me couldn't get enough. I can't wait to see the movie Netflix is making about it. It's gonna be like *The Big Short*, but this time the little guys win.

> You have the power to choose what you value about your-self and others. This isn't about completely throwing out everything you value and forcing yourself to value other things. You're probably closer than you think. You just need to slightly reallocate your attention portfolio. How? By investing in life assets.

Life Assets

Life assets are the things that have value on their own, things you would invest in even if no one else existed. Social currencies are the dividends you get from investing in life assets. Let's break it down:

Life Assets:
- Health (mental, physical, social)
- Creativity
- Growth

Social Currencies:
- Power
- Status
- Beauty

It's not enough to simply tell yourself, "I'm investing attention in my body," because the intention is unclear. There's an unhealthy and healthy way to invest attention in your body.

Rather than investing attention into getting your summer body (social currency of beauty), invest attention into getting your health on track. Health is something that actually has value. It's entirely possible to look great shirtless and be wildly unhealthy. If that's you, you're sacrificing your health in exchange for social currency. This isn't a judgment; it's an observation. I think we've all been there, but you see that being healthy doesn't always mean looking "your best" as much as you want that to be true. Life assets don't always align with social currency the way we expect. However, when you invest attention into your health, you often see social currency dividends.

Creativity is another life asset. Valuing creativity over praise is how you keep your edge in your work without being seduced by the social currency of power, beauty, and status. It's a dangerous one. Whether or not you're an actual artist, you are creative. Everyone creates things. It doesn't have to be music or paintings. Maybe you create really sophisticated excel spreadsheets. Maybe you create spaces where people feel safe sharing their ideas. You create something. Building this life asset looks like investing attention and energy into your art (whatever that is) without the pressure of it being accepted or praised by other people. You would do this even if you were stranded on a deserted island. Did you see *Castaway*? Yeah. He made stuff. Some things he made to preserve his life; other things he made to preserve his humanity. Like Wilson. (Shout out to Tom Hanks, again.)

When you're investing in creativity, your desire is to become better, to continue creating, to experiment, etc. Your desire is not the fame, attention, or approval that might come along with it. Which is great, because then any social currency you get as a result is a bonus. It's free. It's like, you would've done this anyway, so the fact you're getting social validation is like—awesome. But you're not craving it. You're not feeling low if you don't get it.

Also, remember it's okay to give up and try new things. Especially with this one. If you've been creating something for a few years and you don't want to do it anymore, that's okay. Find a new way to express your creativity. You don't owe anyone your creativity. You don't owe anyone your expression. You don't need to stick with the same thing forever just because that's what you started with. Even if you're incredibly famous because of it, you're still allowed to walk away. Remember what I said about quitting? Just give up. Find something new. It's okay.

Growth is the final life asset you can invest your attention into. This looks like education, challenging yourself, and choosing things that aren't always the most comfortable, but in the long run will result in more fulfillment.

This helps you stretch the boundaries of what you think you're capable of. It's important to continue to grow even when you're investing in other life assets. These interests and passions can change, they can evolve, they can die. All of that it okay, as long as you're on a continual path of growth and exploration of who you are. This is how you genuinely live your life. A life filled with things you care about, not a life filled with things that bring nothing more to you than social currency. Again, not that social currency is bad or worthless, but it's an empty reward for the attention and time required to accumulate it.

Invest your time in things you actually value and you will create a meaningful life. That life will come with social currencies, but this form of wealth will be a bonus rather than the focus. That's better than a constant stream of social currency by getting notifications 24/7. That's better than living out someone else's expectations of you.

Exercise: Identify Your Values

Get out that pencil again, because I have a list of questions I'd like you to answer. It may feel tedious to write out your responses but trust me. By answering these questions thoughtfully, you can determine your preferred form of social currency and how you are most likely to judge yourself and others.

1. By what metrics do you usually judge people?

2. What do you currently value, based on where your attention is going?

3. What have you done to impress people? What would you have done if you weren't trying to impress someone?

4. Pretend I gave you an envelope containing a million dollars to create something for yourself. The catch is that it must be entirely for you—not to show anyone, not to make money, not to look impressive. What would you create with that money?

TAKEAWAY

When all's said and done, if you only invest in obtaining more social currency, you aren't actually getting anything tangible. You're just getting validation, but validation isn't satisfying in a lasting way—what you want is something deeper, something meaningful.

Those are the real things in life. Social currency is not time, energy, or resources. It is a placeholder for them. It's a unit to measure them, but it's not the thing itself. It's like looking at a picture of the ocean. You can show someone the ocean is there, but it doesn't capture the full magnitude of experiencing the waves crash against the shore.

CHAPTER 11

Protecting Your Attention

The internet is one of my favorite things. I remember getting my first laptop when I was in high school. I ran up to my room, plugged It In, and typed out "Guess where I am?" in a Facebook message to my best friend.

I couldn't believe I could use the internet while sitting in my bed. What a time to be alive. This was 2009, and I knew it was only going to get better. I was right. I'm not skeptical of new technology; I love it. I think it's fantastic. The fact I can FaceTime with my nephews to watch them grow up even though I'm hours away is incredible. I can learn from master violinists with a quick YouTube search or finding an Instagram page.

Everything is at my fingertips.

The downside to this is that, well, everything is at my fingertips. I can also open my phone to see every single one of the people I went to college with, getting engaged, buying houses, and getting puppies. I can see an endless runway of seemingly perfect women who are "just like me!" getting Starbucks in their Porsches with their perfectly manicured nails and Chanel bags.

I can see people getting their MBA, MD, JD, PhD, and other initials around their name to denote their progression in study.

Then I look around at my life and go, "Wow, I'm so far behind." Or on the days my internal dialogue is harsh, "Wow, I suck."

Where's my luxury lifestyle? Why don't I add some fancy letters to my name? Maybe if I got engaged, I would be as happy as these people look cozied up in their flannel blankets. Maybe I'm not as happy as I thought I was.

And down I go into the spiral of comparing myself to the people I'm exposed to.

"Well, yeah," I think back to myself (internal dialogue, remember?) "of course, you're going to feel down when you compare yourself to 19 different people who look like they're killin' it in 19 different areas. Show me one person who's got it all, all at once, and is actually happy. You can't. Because life doesn't work like that. Having it all looks different to everyone, and no one has the energy to have everything poppin' all at once."

When comparison gets bad, you forget about the life assets you're building and get distracted by other people's social currency. I get it in my head I need to have a Chanel bag and spend my next $6,000 on that instead of investing in the company I'm building.

Why did I do this? Because I thought I needed it. I thought it would make me happy. I thought it was something I "should" have at this point in my life. I thought it would make people think well of me like I thought well of that girl in her Porsche.

When you aren't focusing attention on investing in life assets, you're chasing social currency. That chase lends itself back to comparison because you look at how far you are relative to other people, rather than how close you are to the goal you set for yourself.

When this comparison is happening on a normal scale of a handful of people, it can be "healthy competition." But when it's on the scale of the internet and you have the chance to be exposed to millions of people's progress, stories, and social currency... your pile starts looking pretty small no matter who you are.

But when you no longer use social currency as the measure of your worth, you don't compete. You don't feel inferior. You see her Chanel and think, *Oh, that's gorgeous.* You don't think anything more or less. You don't criticize or fantasize. Your emotional response is low. Your attention is saved, and your energy is contained.

When this stops happening hundreds of times a day, you'll find yourself with an amount of energy that feels overwhelming at first.

This is especially true for body image and the social currency of beauty. The number of times women are conditioned to think about and compare their body to someone else's is astronomical. (By the way, both men and women are impacted by unrealistic body standards, but for the time being I'm going to talk about the female experience because, historically, our society has defined women's identities based on their beauty and physical attributes.)

There's nothing more replaceable than a beautiful woman in Western culture. Think about it. The primary way we measure the worth of a woman is through her looks. If she looks good, we listen to her. But she can't look too good, because then, she must not be credible—clearly, she's been privileged her whole life and doesn't *actually* know what she's talking about. *eyeroll*

Beautiful women are everywhere, and if you're not born that way, you can pay to become that way.

There will always be someone younger. Something different to offer. The standards cultures use to measure beauty change based on time period, location, and even economic factors. If it's a fight you feel like you've won, be prepared to constantly defend the title.

We've seen the beauty icons of the past 60 years come and go. The flowy white dress filled out by the full figure of Marilyn Monroe, the red one-piece swimsuit made famous by the athletic rack of Farrah Fawcett, the boyishly thin Kate Moss, and on to the extreme waist-to-hip ratio of Kim Kardashian.

Over time, beauty expectations evolve slowly, so we don't really notice. Just like how if you put a frog in boiling water, it jumps out, but if you put it in cold water on low heat, it will allow you to boil it without a fight.

Women are the frog. The water is boiling, but you don't realize it unless you feel the contrast.

When you line these body types up next to each other, you see how drastically different they are. From a statistical perspective, these body types would never fall within a standard deviation or two of each other, but at one point, during the past 60 years, each was considered the pinnacle of women's beauty. Each "outlier" body type was a standard every woman felt pressure to meet. Which makes no sense.

And yet, we think the current beauty "standard" is the end all be all of how our body needs to look. Women are rushing out in droves to get lip fillers, breast enhancement surgery, Brazilian Butt Lifts, and rhinoplasty.

If history is any indication, the beauty expectations will change again a few times within my lifetime. (I'm not even calling them beauty standards, because standards don't change.)

If Marilyn lived to see the figure of Kate Moss praised and idolized, she, a former icon herself, would feel dramatically inadequate. Though, perhaps because by that time, her age alone would make her inadequate, culture doesn't mind the unfair shifting expectations. The younger generation is the only one with a chance to meet them, anyway.

No one expects the same woman to keep up with these standards through her life. By the time they change, she's out of her prime and out of the conversation.

How is that even possible? If the icons themselves can't keep up with the changing body ideals of beauty expectations, what chance do any of us have?

A woman could be living through every single one of these "phases" and be completely miserable comparing herself to the shifting expectations unless she magically had the right shape and look during her "prime" years between 21 and 28. Which brings us to the idea of a beauty standard, in general. A standard cannot exist unless it is objective and relatively stable. There is a standard for men's physical appearance but not women's. It's too subjective and changes too frequently to qualify as a standard. At best, it's a fluid cultural idea to personify current fashion trends. At worst, it's an emotional torture device akin to gaslighting that every woman experiences at some level, whether she consents or not.

I joked with my sisters that, "We're just lucky we live during a time when if you've got a booty, people pay attention to you. Cause if we went to high school in the 80s or 90s, no one would think twice about us over our chest."

Were we lucky? Or did we experience a different kind of burden? The attention you get from having the body type everyone wants results in pressure to maintain that body and level of attention. It's just as annoying as striving to reach the desired body type. Both take energy. Both are distracting. Neither get you very far.

When the standard is perfection, embodied like this, everyone falls short. Yes, you can have the chest, but do you have the booty? Okay, you have the booty, but how do you look in a crop top?

Or maybe your body shape is exactly what you see on billboards and Instagram ads, but what are you going to do about those stretch marks? Your crooked nose? Your arm hair? That mole on your stomach?

The amount of body maintenance expected from women by our culture is enough to fill a part-time job, and costs more than what you'd earn working one.

Don't get me wrong, I think physical beauty is a great thing. I also think it's the single biggest waste of energy and cause of anxiety for women today. A frequently-cited 2011 *Glamour* study says 97 percent of women have negative thoughts about their body each day. This is partly due to the constant exposure to edited pictures on the internet but also due to the constant focus and pressure to meet expectations of beauty.

If the standard was always the same, that would be different. So, no, maybe you don't meet the current cultural opinion of the ideal woman's body type. Who cares? They don't even know what they want, so why should you spend time, energy, and attention chasing a moving target?

Oh, and just for the sake of balance, I researched how men's ideal body standards have changed in the past 50-plus years. Spoiler, they haven't.

You'll find listicles saying they have, but the variance is all still within one standard deviation. "Oh, we want more muscle." "Mmm...not that much." "Okay, good." At no point in time did culture tell men, "We want you to be stick thin and short."

It's more about men's fashion changing than their body types, which says a lot about how we view men and women. Women's actual bodies need to change and fit into an ideal. Men just have to wear a different pattern. It's not really about their bodies because we don't talk about men's bodies or study them and critique them the way we do with women.

If you're a tall guy with broad shoulders and a bit of muscle tone, you've been winning for the past 100 years. Just look at every single guy they got to play James Bond. That character has been in movies since 1963, and every actor who's played him had the same body type. Tall, broad shoulders, toned muscles. Daniel Craig came in hot with the glistening abs and hairless chest, but again, that's one standard deviation from the norm.

Yeah, back in the day (like 18th century) it was considered attractive for both men and women to be overweight, but I have a feeling that was more of an "access to food" thing than an "I find this attractive" thing.

Not to say men don't face their own set of issues. When it comes to body image and a sense of attractiveness, no one has it easy. But if we're making comparisons, which it's fair to say we are, the standard deviation in expectations for men are nothing compared to the outlier expectations women are held to from one decade to the next. Which creates an endless cycle of comparison and exposure to changing expectations.

It's one thing to take a look at a standard, know you missed the mark, and move on with your life. It's entirely another thing for the mark to be consistently reinvented before your eyes. Seducing you into believing if you work a little harder, sacrifice a little more, you just might hit it.

The Comparison Complex

When you're overwhelmed by all the success stories in your line of vision, you start thinking you're a total failure. This sabotages our creativity. Instead of making things we like, things we're proud of, etc., we get it in our head we should make things other people will like.

We feel the pressure to share what we're doing so that other people will know the impressive parts of ourselves. Which is why social media feels more like a highlight reel than a behind-the-scenes experience of people's lives (depending on who you follow!)

This turns digital platforms into a liability. You feel pressure to create this online presence that's compelling, but whatever it is, you will need to deliver on that in person. As an introvert, this stresses me out. The sheer number of liabilities demanding my attention, updates, and thoughts. At a certain point, I'm like—no. I'm done sharing. I don't want to participate in the conversation anymore. I'm exhausted.

This is especially true for influencers and content creators. Building a following requires an incredible amount of time, energy, and attention. But the liability doesn't stop once you have a following. Once you have it, you must keep it. You always want to be growing, or at least maintaining your following. This creates a problem as well if you're measuring your worth based on the amount of praise you get through your digital presence. If you're used to tens of thousands of people giving you attention online, it's harder to stay focused and present in person because you know validation is waiting for you on your phone.

You compare yourself to your own progress. But I hope you're starting to see that the way you measure progress is the issue. Does it really matter if you grew your Instagram following to 30,000 in three months if you did it with content you don't care about or believe in? What are people actually following? You—or a fake version of you?

Even if you're not a content creator, just a regular person—hello! You also feel pressure to compare yourself because there are profiles designed to cater to other forms of social currency. LinkedIn is the Mecca for the currencies of status and power.

Get a promotion? Update that status. Posting your professional wins happens on LinkedIn. So you could be a regular person, but comparing yourself to the progress and accomplishments of your professional peers.

Having and not having a digital presence influences how people view you. I've seen people, in an effort to not let their digital presence influence their identity, delete all social media and public accounts. But this also sends a message. Silence and absence send a message. You can't "opt out" of the social currency tied to your digital presence, because choosing to not have one influences how people see you.

But you do have control over how many of these platforms you're willing to participate in. The number of profiles, apps, and platforms you could be trying to maintain is exhausting.

Because, again, the more you have, the more you need to maintain. It's a liability you're creating for yourself. When it feels like you're falling behind, it's easier than ever to fake a little to boost your social currency.

The quick fix is to edit your pictures or profile to appear as though you can keep up with what you're seeing online. You embellish a little here and a little there. You retouch small things at first. Then there's a pressure to deliver on the expectation you created online. When the expectation is realistic and aligned with who you actually are, it's not as stressful. But sometimes, we create a false version of ourselves online. This Frankenstein version that when someone meets us in real life, it's not going to be the same. You create this image of yourself that will earn you more social currency. Maybe you make your captions really clever and funny, but in person you're quiet and can't think on your feet.

Editing your photos gets you more likes? You're gonna keep editing your photos. Eventually, those photos might not even look like you. Then you'll eventually feel pressure to get surgery to make yourself look like the edited version of you.

When you use apps like Facetune and heavily edit pictures on Instagram, you're creating an unsecured liability for yourself. That's why it's causing so much anxiety; you need to maintain this persona in multiple places, plus make good on the persona in person.

This causes stress online and offline because if you run into someone and they don't recognize you, it's essentially discrediting your presence online.

A secured liability is still something you owe. You will still feel like you owe people what you show them online. So even if you really do look like that or you really do have that Rolls, if someone sees you without it, they could claim you're just trying to flex for the 'gram.

There are women posting pictures after spending 40 minutes editing out cellulite, shaping their noses, plumping their lips, and bubbling out their booty. Then you see these pictures and think, *I wish I looked like her.* She wishes the same thing because she doesn't actually look like that. These are unsecured liabilities, and it's stressful to have a profile you need to fake. But it's never too late to decide to stop. Delete the heavily edited photos and just post real pictures of you. You might not get as many likes, but ask yourself why you're posting the picture in the first place.

You get what you put out. If you curate a profile all about your looks, you will attract followers who are all about looks. You are building a house of cards, and when it falls, you have no one to blame but yourself.

You are 100% in charge of how you use social media, who you follow, and what you post. When I realized this, it made me feel powerful. It made me feel in control. I realized it didn't matter if 150 people followed me or 150 million; I would post my real thoughts, my real body, and my real life. Not all of it—there's still plenty I keep private—but I wanted to see and show real stuff. Before this realization, I barely posted anything. I didn't even have Instagram on my phone until 2015. I created an account to share my body image story and post from my podcast, but I realized my followers wanted to know more about my real life, too. So I promised myself I would post regularly to share my thoughts and my life with people interested to know. I wouldn't measure the worth of my social media by my following or number of "likes" but how deeply I impact the people who do follow me.

Each time I get an email or DM about how my podcast or posts helped someone, I'm humbled and encouraged to continue.

But sometimes we get frustrated with Instagram. We get annoyed with what we see, how our posts "perform." Why? If you're annoyed by anything, be annoyed by what you're allowing in your digital space. Be annoyed with what you're creating in your digital space. Take full accountability for it and make changes if you need to. Be aware of what you're comparing yourself to and why you think you're lacking in some way. Remember, so much of what you see is fake, anyway. So don't worry about it.

Action Step

If you're trying to stop comparing yourself, you need to decrease your exposure to social currency. When you lower the opportunities to compare yourself, you'll naturally do it less.

So, if you're one of the 500 million people on Instagram every day, go ahead and hide the "like" count in your settings. This is a genius feature that instantly separates content from its social currency. Here's how to do it: Under settings > privacy > posts, you can toggle to Hide Like and View Counts. This makes it so you cannot see the number of likes and views on content. You can restrict if other people see the number of likes and views on your posts in each individual post, under advanced settings.

Instead of watching a video because it has 50,000 likes, you don't see how many people like it. You choose to watch, read, or scroll away based on what it's actually about. People like what other people like; we're interested in what's popular. So if you don't know what's popular, even on your own feed, that helps you make choices based on what's genuinely interesting to you.

This also clearly removes the ability to compare how many likes your post got versus the ones you see in your feed. It just says "liked by **rebekahbuege** and **others**." Isn't that crazy? You literally don't know exactly how many people liked the post.

The competition is essentially gone. It hides the "social currency" of that post. You don't see how much attention or approval it got. You get to make the choice for yourself if you like it or not, without being influenced by the value of its social currency.

TAKEAWAY

When I took this step, it helped me feel normal again. I'm not distracted by questions like, "Why does this have so many likes?" or "How do I get more people to like my posts?" when I'm on Instagram.

I don't get annoyed anymore if a stupid post got 100,000 likes. Because I just don't see it. There's no opportunity for me to compare, because it's gone. And that brings me peace.

CHAPTER 12

Stop Blaming Technology

Look at your average screen time per day. I'm happy to say mine is around four hours currently. But that's just on my iPhone. Most of my day is spent looking at the laptop screen. I'm one of those normal people who loves TV. I'm heavily invested in the characters of *Grey's Anatomy*, *The Office*, and recently got sucked into *Outlander* (and Sam Heughan).

If I'm conscious for 15 hours a day, four are spent on my phone, six are spent on my laptops, and two are spent watching TV. The rest is invested in my morning routine, going for walks, practicing violin, rock climbing, spending face-to-face time with friends, etc. Practically my entire day, except three hours, is spent immersed in a digital world.

No wonder I care what my online presence looks like. No wonder I stress over if my Instagram looks good. No wonder I want to look good online.

That's where "everything" happens. That's still where most of my attention and energy is going…and I've detoxed my notifications. I'm in control of my digital use—it's not addictive anymore or pulling me away from my focus—but I'm still showing up there.

I'm not saying investing attention into digital spaces is bad. I'm not saying you can't invest in life assets when your attention is focused on a digital space. Like I said, in this digital world, that's where everything happens.

For example, I spend time recording and producing my podcast, serving clients, responding to voice notes from clients, going live on Instagram and teaching a helpful concept, texting friends, going on FaceTime with my parents... even writing this book is attention spent in a digital space.

So that's not to say any time spent in digital space is time spent pursuing social currency; it's just that these spaces are where social currency is traded the most and valued the highest. It's easy to judge and measure people online.

You're exposed to high amounts of social currency when you're in digital spaces because the access you have to profiles is unlimited. You're always reminded of that base level desire for more and the anxiety of losing what you have. But this exposure isn't always accurate. Remember the amount of "faking it" you personally do (or should I say, *did*) and extrapolate that across the billion accounts online that can easily do the same thing.

Digital distortion doesn't tell the whole story. It makes it look like something is popular, beautiful, powerful, or important when it might not be. This digital resume is separate from you, though. It's not who you are. It's a representation of parts of you. You leave that behind every time you interact with someone in real life. The digital representation of you isn't real. The validation of the digital representation of you isn't enough to satisfy your desire for worthiness.

Social currency isn't enough to fulfill your need for significance. Just like money cannot fill your need for nourishment; you need to use it to buy food. You can use social currency to "buy" what you truly need. Getting attention is the beginning of any connection. Someone needs to give you attention before you can know them. So savvy social currency traders use that to link them with someone else. You can find what you have in common with someone and use that to form a connection. This will be covered in detail in a later chapter, but if you have an interest in music and some talent there (social currency of beauty) and you meet a musician, that social currency will be valued in their eyes and that can earn you a connection.

By now, we've covered what brings purpose to your life. You need to enjoy, express, and connect with yourself, others, and the world.

You can use the attention you get from your talent, for example, to meet new people, form new friendships, and create connections. You can use the attention you get from your associations to do the same. Taking those connections offline is one way to make them more potent in your life. I'm not discrediting the value of online forums, groups, and spaces— they can be supportive and community focused. But take an active role in reminding yourself you're not alone in the physical world.

The only reason you think your digital presence is everything is because that's what you're paying attention to most. The less you pay attention to your phone, email, and general digital world, the more you realize there is to enjoy in the physical world. There's literally so much to enjoy in real life. There are so many ways to express yourself in real life. There are so many ways to form genuine connections in real life.

In fact, genuine connection is even more potent than ever before. With the increase in attention paid to screens, if you have someone's attention in person, it's all the more valuable. It's rare. It's hard to get people to leave their house and do something in person because we have more available on-demand—or delivered within the hour—than other generations had available in their lifetimes.

Even if a person is physically there with you in person, it doesn't mean you have their attention. These phones are constantly bidding for our attention—which is why I told you to turn off your notifications a few chapters back. They break your attention and reduce your enjoyment of the present moment. While it's hard to get people to go out and do things, they still want to.

With this increase in availability of digital entertainment, there's an increase in the intensity of desire for in-person connection.

Maybe the overall demand for entertainment has been met by the digital world, but the intensity of the demand for in-person connection is increasing. Coming out of the COVID-19 quarantine, people are hungry for live music, live shows, etc. They want to go to the movie theater instead of stream on Netflix, because it wasn't an option for over a year.

Think of it this way. The potential influence you have over the people you interact with in person has more impact than any digital presence you might have. Regardless of your following or clout online, the connections you have in person are more impactful because people have fewer of them. I see maybe four people in a given day. But I follow over a hundred accounts on Instagram. The people I see in person have more of an impact than the people I see online. I translate that into creating a bigger impact on people I get the chance to meet in real life.

One of my favorite ways to make an impression in person is through small, thoughtful gifts. I surprise my friends with home-made banana bread. I forget about my ego and ask people to do things—go on hikes, get coffee, etc. I offer to help with things they're working on.

If you only have followers online but no real friends in person, it feels empty. That's not the fault of technology—it's on you for investing more attention in your phone than in-person interactions.

You have more impact on the real world than you think you do. Your digital influence is only one part of who you are. You have opportunities every day to make in-person connections with people in your life. Even if they aren't "main characters" in your life (yet), you can practice investing energy in people.

> Act like you have an impact. I don't mean "fake it 'til you make it." I mean be the person you already are. Invest richly in the people you see each day.

Action Steps to Be Present

1. **Be mindful and intentional about how you walk into a room.** Your phone should be out of hand and out of sight. Give your full attention to the room as you enter it. Notice how the room is arranged, where people are gathered, etc.

2. **Give your full attention to the person speaking to you.** Think more deeply about who they are; don't just focus on what they think of you. The more attention you give someone, the more impact you have on them. I don't mean attention over time. I mean the potency of attention you give someone in the moment. That means your eyes, ears, and thoughts are only on them.

3. **Don't multitask.** You might think it helps you be more efficient, but life isn't about efficiency, remember? It's about enjoyment, expression, and connection. Multitasking in social situations dilutes your attention and energy. When you appear distracted, you make the people around you feel unworthy of your full attention. Making people feel unworthy is a garbage way to influence them. It can work, but only on people desperate for approval—and I don't know about you, but I don't want to attract desperate people into my life. I want to attract whole, confident, secure people who like me for who I am and have the capacity to pour into me the way I pour into them.

4. **Resist the urge to check your phone.** Subconsciously, you may think it makes you look busy and important, but in reality, it just robs you of the opportunity to be present with the people around you.

5. **Ask questions. And then shut up and listen.** Giving others your full attention, your full energy, and your full time will impact people more than you can imagine. This is because influence happens when someone feels like you care about them. Fair warning, this won't be reciprocated by people who are caught up in social currency and addicted to their phones. However, the people who notice your full attention won't know what to do with it all. They might confuse your attention with infatuation. I've been on several first dates where the guy was surprised to find out I wasn't interested in date number two. They were convinced we had a "rare" connection, but really all I did was give my full attention. Even though not everyone will reciprocate this level of attention, confident, secure people will be able to reciprocate in ways you will appreciate.

6. **Take your time. Slow down.** Doing things slowly helps you do them right the first time. People who are calm and collected don't give off desperate energy. People are attracted to that. You also don't waste attention bouncing between multiple things at once. Save that attention. Save that energy.

CHAPTER 13

Diversifying Your Social Currency Holdings

There's a difference between a currency being declined and being completely devalued. My beauty currency was first devalued when I was 20 years old. I competed in the forensic circuit in college. This isn't where you test particle samples for gunshot residue and link DNA to a murder suspect like on *CSI Miami*. Forensics, in this case, is where hundreds of college kids get dressed to the nines at 6:00 a.m. on weekends. I'm talking full suits, hair, and makeup. Then they perform and compete against each other in interpretation, public address, and limited-preparation speech events.

Yeah, I was that kid.

Before ever entering a conference room in my corporate life, I was rocking a red power suit every weekend complete with pantyhose, high heels, and pearl earrings, my hair teased back into a voluminous yet sleek straight ponytail. My speech partner-in-crime benevolently called it the "b*tch bump"—and it was.

No one was prepared for the power of the b*tch bump. Every time It showed up, a few trophies were sure to follow.

These were my people for four years. Students attended from across the country, from every background you could imagine— privileged perfectionists (me) to impoverished improvisers. It didn't matter who you were outside that room; all that mattered was what you did with the 10 minutes you had to impress the judges with your speech.

As a beautiful, straight white woman, I found that it was one of the only communities in which I had to work harder to be liked and accepted. I felt prejudice because of the way I looked, which was weird because usually that's why people accepted me.

Most of the guys were gay—the girls, too—so it put me in this situation where the type of beauty I had wasn't appealing to the majority of people I was with. This led me to experience a sense of relief and also confusion. During one of the late-night van rides back to the Minnesota State University Campus, I remember blurting in a moment of unedited honesty as I reflected on the panel of gay men I tried to impress in my last round of competition, "I'm not used to being around people who aren't sexually attracted to me or intimidated by me. I couldn't get a read on any of them!"

Not everyone appreciated that comment the way I intended it. That wasn't coming from a place of arrogance (although, that's how one teammate chose to interpret it); it was just true. For the first time in my life, I was in a room full of men who clearly didn't have a sexual agenda when it came to evaluating me as a human, performer, or otherwise. I was surprised to say it felt nice.

There's an unexpected upshot to your social currency being completely devalued in a social setting. You're forced to be more than that. You have to search for the other things that make you who you are. You can't ride out your looks, power, or status when nobody cares. I couldn't rest on "maybe the judge will think I'm hot" to secure my first-place trophy.

When you understand your own social currency, you can use it more effectively. You can also tell the type of currency other people value, whether they're aware of it or not. When you know this, it's easier to show the currency they most readily accept. For example, if you realize you only carry the social currency of beauty, you can invest time and effort into expanding your power and status. That way, if you're in the room with someone who values power over beauty, you can show that currency in that transaction.

Women are often stereotyped for being empty headed but beautiful. This is an example of leaning too heavily in one social currency. You might be beautiful, but if you want to be valued in more circles, you need to diversify your holdings. People will still make this assumption of you, but don't let them be right!

Life Assets as the Key to Diversification

One tried and true way to diversify your social currency is to establish, develop, and then tap into your life assets. When you invest in a skill, you get attention from that talent, and that attention translates to social currency. So it stands to reason that the more skills, talents, and life assets that you put time into, the more you will get back out in social currency.

Don't get me wrong. I'm not saying you should develop life assets with the sole purpose of increasing or diversifying your social currency. That leads to the trap we've already discussed earlier in the book—the endless chase for success despite feelings of emptiness. No, your reasons for developing life assets should be to find joy and/or meaning. If you decide to learn to play the guitar, for example, it should be simply because you adore music and want to be able to play the songs you've always loved. But the better you get—the more you develop the life asset—the more attention you're bound to attract because of it. The more you do this in different areas of your life, the more you will have unintentionally diversified your social currency holdings.

Tree People Versus Forest People

In my first job out of college I worked as a sales development representative for a cloud software company in downtown Minneapolis. My manager, Andre, was a big fan of podcasts (probably because of his 90-minute commute to the office, one way). One morning, he stood up as I walked toward my cube and said, "I know the problem." I hadn't even taken my jacket off before he was leaning over the partition in the way only my favorite co-workers felt comfortable doing.

We were stalled in a deal that was taking all our energy to move forward. We even went on site to visit the headquarters in L.A. (my first time there) and made zero progress.

"I was listening to this podcast on the way in," he continued, "and they were talking about forest people and tree people. It's your perspective on a situation. Do you see the forest or the individual trees? If you're too focused on the trees, you lose sight of the fact it's part of a bigger system. We're talking to a tree person; we need a forest person."

From that day onward, we categorized prospects into tree person or forest person. We needed to align with forest people—the people who saw the bigger picture and didn't let the pieces distract them from the puzzle they were putting together. The purpose of a tree is to make up a forest. The purpose of a puzzle piece is to create a picture. And the purpose of any currency is to use it for some kind of increase in pleasure or decrease in pain. It's a tool used to increase our happiness.

If your pursuit of social currency is decreasing your happiness in a macro sense, you're losing sight of the forest for the trees. So go ahead and put yourself to the test. Are you a forest person or a tree person?

Using your social currency to obtain more social currency or even swap out one for another is like using Monopoly money to buy houses and hotels on Park Place. It helps you in the game, but you're still playing Monopoly. Even winning that game earns you nothing more than a moment of respect before returning to real life. You aren't gaining anything of real value.

Social currency itself doesn't help you in real life unless you use it for its intended purpose. The purpose of social currency is to bring you closer to other people, to help you connect, to help you express, and to help you enjoy yourself and the company of other people.

Ironically, when we try to accumulate currency for the sake of currency, we get further from people. We don't want them to see who we truly are, just the currency we feel comfortable showing.

Vulnerability is the only thing that brings people closer together. This currency is a tool that can open the door to vulnerable connections or create a wall to ensure that never happens. The choice is yours.

You can bank on your social currency—or you can build social wealth—depending on how willing you are to be vulnerable.

The Life Assets We're Born With: Body, Mind, and Heart

Every person, no matter their economic background, family, or other variable, has three life assets in which they can invest attention, time, and energy. You have your body, your mind, and your heart.

You will always have those three things no matter how much social currency you have or relational equity you build. Those are the true elements that make up a person. Not how many Instagram followers, subscribers, or retweets you get online. It's not how many job offers you get (or don't get). It's not how much money you make (or don't make).

The quality of your life depends on the health and expansion of your inherent assets, which is why when you invest energy into education, it's rewarding only if you're doing it to expand your mind. When you do it for the sake of social currency, you're drained by the work, and no matter how many degrees or achievements you have, it never seems to be enough because you can always compare it to someone who has something more impressive.

Action Steps

Once you know what's important, spend time and attention training yourself to invest properly.

1. Use an attention-training app like Headspace, Calm, or Abide to focus your thoughts.

2. Listen to my podcast, *Confidently She*.

3. Get the right people in your life and voices in your head that help you focus on building life assets in a way that's sustainable, not a way where you'll burn out.

CHAPTER 14

No Rewards Without Risk

The first time I went to a movie alone, it was out of righteous indignation. My ex-boyfriend cancelled our plans to see *Maleficent* last minute because he wanted to go to happy hour with his coworkers. We were on the rocks for months, I was looking forward to seeing this movie all week, and his careless cancellation was the final straw. But I figured, you know what? I want to see this movie. If this guy isn't going to come with me, I'm going to see it by myself. As I slipped on my boots and grabbed my car keys, I was determined not to let him—or anyone—stop me from having a good time.

But the closer I got to the theater, the more anxiety settled in. *What if people realize I'm there alone? What will they think of me? Will I look like a loser sitting there all by myself? And what about standing in line to get my ticket—should I pretend like I'm texting someone who's on their way or embrace the shame of not having anyone to go with?*

The minute I opened the theater doors and felt the cool blast of air conditioning, it was like a light bulb went off in my head. *Guess what? Nobody here cares. No one is paying attention to me.*

I walked right up to the ticket counter and purchased a single ticket. The guy behind the glass didn't give me the weird look I was expecting. Next, I walked to the snack counter and ordered a large Sprite and regular popcorn. Nobody raised their eyebrows in judgement. In fact, nobody was looking at me at all. And you know what? It felt great. I felt free for the first time in months. I picked the exact seat I wanted and got comfortable. The screen lit up as the room darkened. I felt a chill down my spine and realized, *I'm here just for myself.* I laughed at the parts of the movie I thought were funny, not just to join in with my boyfriend laughing. No one got mad at me for laughing too loudly. No one complained about my snack choices. No one missed important plot points I had to later explain to them. I got to sit there and fully enjoy the movie I had been looking forward to seeing for weeks.

Going to the movie alone was a social risk for me—any time you push past your social comfort zone, it constitutes a social currency risk—but it paid off, big-time. After that, I started doing more things on my own that I used to feel strange doing without company. I go to nice dinners alone. I go to museums alone. I even take vacations alone. I learned to enjoy my own company so I wouldn't miss out on life experiences just because my friends were busy. I experimented with things, started small, and figured out what I actually liked, instead of what I did only to accommodate the preferences of the people I care about.

As any financial advisor will tell you, there is no reward without risk. Whether it's real estate, precious metals, or the stock market, you must take a risk if there's going to be a reward. The same is true when it comes to social investments. You're going to have to be okay with taking a little (or a big) social currency risk if you want to have a flourishing relational and experiential portfolio.

Risk as Investment Strategy

Risks come in all shapes and sizes.

My indignant experiment with solo movie-going represented a small risk, where the only thing really at stake was my pride. Larger social currency risks include asking for someone's number, introducing yourself to a celebrity or executive in the elevator, or running through the airport to make the only direct flight from LAX to Rapid City that week. All risks I've taken with varying degrees of social success.

Throughout my life I have also taken substantial social currency risks that put my income and professional reputation on the line. Anyone who decides to leave an office job with benefits to start their own business is inherently walking into the unknown, and the consequences of a risk like this are significant. There were days when I didn't know if I was making a smart choice or not, but I committed to the risk for one simple reason: I knew that if I stayed in the corporate world, I would always wonder if I would've been happier going off on my own.

I was lucky (hard work helped), and my risk resulted in a meaningful reward: a dynamic career that I love. But the thing about risks is that while some pay off, most don't. You must be prepared for when things don't go according to plan. You have to afford to lose short-term social currency if you want to make long-term gains in life assets.

The difference is, I believe the time you spend investing in your life assets is never truly wasted. That's because life assets—things like your health, your passion projects, and your most important relationships—will be there for you regardless of the ebbs and flows of your social currency balance.

Let's say you have a passion for whiskey, and you decide to take a risk by starting a YouTube channel about whiskey tasting, distilleries, and the best places to travel for a whiskey experience. On the one hand, this risk might result in an ultimatum from your day job because your boss feels your new hobby isn't a good representation of the company and you're "losing focus" on work. Even if that happens and you choose to give it up, that doesn't necessarily mean the time you spent nurturing your passion was time wasted. On the other hand, your risk may end up paying dividends down the road (e.g., you may land a brand deal with Jack Daniel's that leads to a new career entirely centered on something you love). Moreover, the connections you form with your subscribers and fans might be a reward in itself. Knowing you're educating people and providing a source of entertainment is rewarding, too. The point is, when you invest attention into life assets—which hold their value regardless of social currency—you mitigate your long term risk by creating opportunities for other types of rewards.

Taking Risks Sooner Rather Than Later

The sooner you take a risk, the sooner you'll know if it pays off. Likewise, the time you spend contemplating the risk—putting it off because of fear—is time you won't be able to spend enjoying the payoff if it works out.

I learned this lesson in a small way back in seventh grade, during a pool party I'll never forget. All my friends were having a diving contest, and I'd never learned to dive. I could jump off the diving board, sure, but headfirst? No way. It didn't matter that I was 13 years old and everyone was doing it. I was terrified.

But I wasn't just afraid of the physical injury that might result in doing it wrong. I was afraid everyone would laugh at me for doing it wrong. That created more fear in my body than the many hospital scenarios running through my head.

Eventually, word got out that I didn't know how to dive. All my friends were super nice, no pressure, offering to teach me, and I still said no. I waited until the very last possible opportunity to try. I figured this way, I could leave the party immediately if I was embarrassed. I dove in like my friend taught me, hands over my head, into the pool.

As I plunged into the water, I felt a rush of pride and regret at the same time. I gulped for air as I resurfaced, wiped the water from my eyes, and thought to myself, *I've been missing out on this fun the whole time.*

I loved it. If I would've just tried it sooner, I would've been able to practice and enjoy diving with my friends for the whole party instead of trying at the last minute when my parents were already on their way to pick me up.

What fun have you been missing out on this whole time?

Fear is a funny thing. There are so many things we hold ourselves back from because we're afraid people will make fun of us, think we're stupid, or laugh when we fail. The thing is, you do lose social currency when you fail. I'm not going to say there's no consequence.

People who judge you in a shallow way will reject you for trying something and failing. But if you don't try things, you'll never live the life you truly want. The path of safety never leads anywhere interesting. Also, what does safety really look like? Nothing is safe. Nothing is guaranteed.

One of the things I realized I was missing out on (besides diving at my friend's 13th birthday party) was enjoying things I like because I didn't want to be judged.

For example, I like fancy things.

I love a good YSL bag, I like Fendi, Alexander McQueen, and my Tiffany earrings are one of my prized possessions. I genuinely like those things. I used to resist wanting them or admitting I liked them because I thought people would write me off as a snob or materialistic.

But after self-reflection, I found my heart in the matter was not from a sense of superiority or shallow consumerism. I was drawn to the aesthetic, quality, and artistic value in these designer items. By denying myself those things I could easily afford, I was allowing myself to be limited by other people's hypothetical assumptions and perceptions of me. Again, no one is paying attention to you as much as you think they are. You have permission to like the things you like, but always ask yourself first, "Why do I like this? What do I like about it?" and go from there.

Why do I like Tiffany's? Because I like timeless looks and elegance, and that's the Tiffany's brand. I like spending money on myself, and I like knowing that my jewelry meets a high standard of quality. What I *don't* do is go around telling everyone my earrings are from Tiffany's. (I realize the irony of including this in the book, but how else am I supposed to give this example? Haha.)

So go ahead and ask yourself what you've been missing out on. What things—whether objects, people, or experiences—have you been depriving yourself of due to fear of judgment or shame? If you're like most of my clients, you may find yourself with a list that's longer than you'd care to admit. I want you to study that list carefully and then genuinely ask yourself: "What's the worst thing that could happen if I took a little risk and embraced these things?"

Getting Used to Taking Risks

The secret to getting comfortable with risk-taking is breaking your attachment to social currency. This way, when you suddenly find yourself in situations where your currency is at risk, you don't care. You aren't as attached to that being part of your identity, so you can easily pivot, secure in the knowledge that your life assets are valuable regardless of the ups and downs of your social currency.

To practice this, you'll need to break your pattern of social currency on purpose. In other words, I want you to intentionally/artificially try to lower your currency and see what happens. Test out your fears and see how you cope. If you stress over your outfit looking perfect, intentionally wear something that doesn't match. This helps release your attachment to the social currency you crave and prove to yourself no one really cares as much as you think they do.

One thing I started doing is dancing and singing along to my music while I take my daily walks. I enjoy myself—and I don't care if anyone sees me or thinks I'm weird. I'm having fun—and I'm not out here to look cool in front of strangers. Because life is about enjoyment, expression, and connection. It's not about getting people to think you're cool. Cool for what? Exactly.

Action Steps

The purpose of this exercise is to force yourself to intentionally do something that feels uncomfortable, so I want you to pick whichever challenge feels most awkward to you:

1. Eat out at a restaurant alone. (Don't stare at your phone the whole time.)

2. Take a page from Rebekah in 2014 and catch a movie on your own.

3. If fashion is your jam, wear that outfit in your closet you've been avoiding because "you can't pull it off" to your next small social event. I bet someone compliments you if you wear it with confidence.

4. If you're a person whose career is core to your identity, tell someone you have a career you would hate—like a telemarketer or hedge fund manager or yoga teacher. Whatever would make you embarrassed, just say it the next time you meet someone you're never going to see again.

TAKEAWAY

So how did it go? Did the world crumble? Did you melt into a puddle of embarrassment? Did you instantly lose thousands of IG followers?

Or did taking a risk in the social department simply prove to you that people are paying a lot less attention to you than you think? I have a feeling I know the answer.

CHAPTER 15

Common Investment Mistakes

If you've been faithfully following the recommendations in this book—turning off notifications, setting boundaries, and learning to take calculated risks to prioritize your life assets—you may have already started to notice changes in your day-to-day attention-spending patterns. That's because when you follow these steps, you're likely to experience a surplus of energy, focus, and time.

Problem solved, right?

Not so fast. The thing about having time and attention to spare is that it doesn't always feel as natural as you expect. It feels weird at first—like you're missing something. (That's social currency withdrawal. You miss it, you think about it constantly, and you wonder if you still have it.) Having time to spare may even boost your anxiety level by giving you a sense of expectation and pressure. After all, you don't want to waste your newfound surplus.

It reminds me of when I first had enough money in the bank to make some investments. I froze. For the first time, it was up to me to decide where my money went. I knew I didn't want to frivolously spend it on something flashy, but what was I supposed to do with it? I didn't want to let it sit in the bank, I didn't want to blindly invest in the stock market, but I didn't know exactly where to put it.

The same thing happens when you have attention and energy to spare, and if you're like most people, you make the same four mistakes before you learn to invest it wisely. But unlike most people, you have the luxury of learning them now so you can avoid them and invest that attention wisely from the jump.

Mistake #1:
Falling Back Into Old Patterns

Habits are hard to break. If you roll over in bed every single morning and scroll through Instagram before even getting up to go pee, chances are that no amount of silencing your notifications is going to magically snap you out of that morning routine. If you're used to laughing at TikToks on the toilet (we've all been there), you need some serious willpower when you walk into that bathroom to make sure you get out of there before your legs go numb.

Nearly everyone who embarks on the process of investing their attention more thoughtfully goes through periods where they relapse into their old patterns. I'm not just talking about social media habits, but also patterns of thought—namely the automatic way we size people up and make judgments about who they are and what we want from them. The same goes for the thought patterns we have about ourselves—including negative self-talk, self-doubt, and the persistent belief that other people are more interesting or worthy of attention than we, ourselves, are.

Fortunately, slipping back into old patterns every now and then does not mean all is lost. Your efforts are not in vain. Each time you notice yourself engaging in an old habit, be gentle with yourself and say out loud what's happening. "Oh, I'm assuming this person driving the Rolls Royce in front of me is wealthy…now I'm feeling insecure about my Mercedes…I shouldn't assume they're wealthy. They might not even own that car. Their car has nothing to do with my car and I'm thankful for what I have." And treat at it as an opportunity to practice shifting your attention towards something worthy of your investment.

Mistake #2:
Launching Yourself into
Hyper-Productivity Mode

This next mistake is one I'm familiar with. The constant pressure to maximize every moment, to be ruthlessly efficient with your time, and to turn yourself into a machine with one goal above all others: productivity.

How many times have you found yourself with a free hour and decided to spend it sorting and moving files on your computer ("I'm going to finally get organized!") or sorting and moving piles throughout your house ("I'm going to finally Marie Kondo this crap!")? How many times have you said to yourself, "If I only had a little extra time, I'd go to the gym every day and get into the best shape of my life!" When the pandemic hit in 2020, how many of you decided to double-down on some goal you'd had for a long time, like, "Now I'm going to finally write that book!" (Okay, I'm glad I followed through on that one.)

My point is, ever since the Puritans landed on our shores touting their famous work ethic, American culture has been obsessed with productivity. We're taught in so many subtle (and not-so-subtle) ways that to be idle is to be lazy, or even a sin. We're encouraged to spend every spare minute doing more, being more, and achieving more.

Not only that—we're taught to maximize our efficiency while being productive, multi-tasking to complete more than one goal at the same time. How many times have you listened to a podcast while simultaneously loading the dishwasher and periodically shouting at Alexa to add items to your shopping list? No wonder we are all exhausted. The amount of pressure we put on ourselves to maximize every moment of even "spare time" has reached ridiculous new heights in the age of the internet.

It took me some trial and error to figure this out.

When I first felt this "extra" time in my life, I wanted to make the most of it. That's the natural instinct, at least in this highly capitalist country. So I picked up new hobbies, expanded my social life, joined a Thursday night beach volleyball league and Tuesday rock climbing. I filled the time. I used the energy.

But eventually, that got me back to the same problem. My attention was always on something, at the end of every day, I was still exhausted. At the beginning of every day, I felt like I had no time. My emotional, physical, and spiritual reserves were constantly depleted.

As humbling as it was to realize I had lost my surplus, the experience led me to an important realization: I needed to take a break. I needed to give myself permission, once and for all, to do absolutely nothing productive with my "spare" time and attention.

Mistake #3:
Mistaking Entertainment for Rest

The most radical way to invest a surplus of time, energy, and attention is to rest. Unfortunately, for most of us, we confuse rest with being passively entertained. We put on comfy clothes, grab the remote, and kick back to watch the latest Netflix series.

When I realized that I needed to take a break, I made this mistake. One week I binged an entire season of *Outlander* before it struck me that binging television was A) another symptom of our culture's obsession with maximizing, and B) not all that restful to my mind, body, or spirit.

Here's the thing, entertainment is just another way of distracting yourself. When you're watching a big screen or a small one in your hand, your brain is not resting—it's being passively stimulated. And I hate to break it to you, but you can't rest and be entertained at the same time, no matter how much of a dopamine hit your brain gets every time you click "next episode." That's not entering into deep rest.

The key difference between rest and passive entertainment is that rest consists of time intentionally spent in solitude. In quiet.

Alone with your thoughts. Reconnecting with your mind, body, and heart.

This means exercising without music in your ears. It means going for a walk without listening to a podcast. It means learning to be comfortable in your own skin, with no one's company but yourself.

Does this sound boring? Does it scare you? If you find yourself feeling resistant, check in with yourself and ask why. You may be avoiding something that needs to be addressed before you can allow this rest to be fully restorative.

Mistake #4:
Believing You Owe Someone
Your Attention or Energy

It took me a few years to learn that I don't owe my employer, my followers, or my clients *all* my attention and energy. Being a valuable employee doesn't mean responding to emails at 9:00 p.m. on a Wednesday. Being a valuable influencer doesn't mean sharing every second of my life. Being a valuable coach doesn't mean taking calls on the weekends. Just because technology gives you the ability to be reached anywhere at anytime, doesn't mean you should allow it. This can get especially unhealthy in your career.

You don't owe work (whatever that is for you) access to you all the time. Even during "work hours," you can time block and put boundaries around what you focus on and when. You can choose to check your email twice a day. You can choose to only have meetings in the morning or afternoon and use other times of the day for administrative or prep work. This protects your attention from being broken during the times you need to focus on creating a presentation, writing an email, drafting a contract, etc. All your work will be waiting for you. There's a lot of false urgency created by the instant nature of our communication.

The same goes with your friends and family. You don't owe them unlimited, immediate access to your attention and energy either. If someone is bringing drama into your life, you get to decide when to take a step back, when to turn down that invitation for coffee, and when to decline a request for help. If your sister texts you in a panic at 1:00 a.m. because her toxic boyfriend hasn't come home from the bar, you don't need to drop everything to comfort her for the 19th time. You can respond on your own time and help in a way that works for you.

Drawing these attention boundaries is important in protecting your energy. But that feeling of being needed and essential pays into our feeling of worth. It makes us feel like we have status in that person's life and are important to them. Setting boundaries with people helps you see if this is actually true. If someone respects your boundary, you are important to them. If someone disrespects your boundary, you are a vehicle for them to get their needs met. While it's painful, they will soon move on to finding someone else who will let them get away with it. But you don't want keep these energy vampires in your life, even if it gives a source of shallow validation.

When you don't crave that validation, it's easier to set the boundary and fully invest your attention in healthy relationships.

Taking Control of Your Investments with an Attention Balance Sheet

To recap, the ways your attention can be stolen, divided, and diluted are at an all-time high. There's your phone, which in itself has dozens of attention banks you can pay into. Other attention banks include TV, video games, work, our own bodies (hunger requires immediate attention), social obligations, and just about anything that stimulates one or more of your five senses.

But some of these attention banks are one-way streets. You deposit attention, and there is no withdrawal. A lot of the things we do on our phones, every day, are examples of this. Every time I see someone on their phone, I can't help but wonder what has their attention. Is it something that's going to make them smarter? Are they connecting with a friend? is it purely entertainment? I have begun asking myself the same question when I notice myself reaching for my own phone on autopilot. What am I looking for? Why am I breaking my focus?

To take control of my attention addiction, I decided to take inventory of where my attention was going and the things I wanted to create space for. An attention balance sheet, if you will. Your personal balance sheet consists of the daily energy and attention investments you make. Every day you have energy, time, and attention. Energy is not a constant, so we will set that aside for now.

Time isn't completely within your control. Some days you have more free time than others. You can save time by multitasking or make time by rescheduling or canceling plans. But your attention is different. You can't save your attention. You can't make room for attention. You always have attention to give, and it must be spent on something.

Let's say your day is broken into 100 units of attention. You use all 100 units per day—but you never run out.

Your personal balance sheet is made up of what you give your attention units to each day, each week, each month, for your entire life. You cannot change this. You cannot get a refund for attention wasted on something you didn't get an ROI on. There are no returns or exchanges. How you spend it is set in stone.

Scary? Yes. Motivating? Even more, yes.

You can't change what you paid attention to in the past, so there's no point in regretting any of it. Remember, focus on what you can control. The good news is you can control what you pay attention to going forward. It starts by tracking where your attention currently goes. That means reflecting on the past few months, or even years, to get a sense of your balance sheet.

Think of it like the transactions on your credit card. Each day, reflect on your attention "balance sheet" and keep track of how it changes as you read this book. You can use broad categories or track it hour by hour. If you're a "chapter-a-day" reader, use these last few chapters to hold yourself accountable and reflect on where your attention goes over the next few days.

Setting Attention Boundaries

When I started going into an office again after being self-employed for three years, it was tough. I used to set my own schedule; now I had to be in by 8:30 a.m. Rather than salvaging every minute of sleep I could get, I went the other way. I took control of my mornings and woke up at 6:00 a.m. to spend a full hour enjoying a cup of coffee, journaling, and reading my Bible. I didn't even look at my phone until 7:30 a.m. when I was about to shower and get ready to leave.

This "unreachable" time in the morning gives me clarity. It protects me from any stress hitting me first thing when I open my eyes.

Think about it. If there's an email with bad news waiting for me, I won't see it until I get to the office at 8:30 a.m. (boundaries). If there's a text from my sister about a fight she got into with her boyfriend, I won't see that until 7:30 a.m., before I get into the shower.

I have that solid, protected hour alone with my thoughts and God to center myself and face the day. I can breathe. I start the day responding to whatever comes my way, not impulsively reacting to news as it comes.

To upgrade this experience further, I got a Hatch alarm clock. This is an incredible device you pair with the Hatch app. While setting it up, you're supposed to give it a name. While I'm not one to name inanimate objects, I decided to have some fun. Instead of "Rebekah's Hatch" or "Bedroom," I chose Jasper.

Jasper is more than an alarm clock. He creates a bedtime routine complete with a timed reading light, breathwork practice, and white noise while I sleep. Then, in the morning (this is my favorite), he mimics the sunrise for 30 minutes. Once the "sun" is up, my chosen sound chimes the alarm. I chose a Malibu Sunrise with Mountain Alps sound as the alarm. I feel like Cinderella waking up to the birds singing at her window as the sun shines in.

The best part? My phone is across my bedroom on the charger. Out of reach. Out of sight. Out of mind. I can snooze the alarm, shut it off, and start my day without ever touching my phone. Then I can do my morning routine—journaling, coffee, and prayer—without any temptation of social currency, external validation, or bad news ruining a perfectly good morning.

Every day has the possibility to be peaceful and intentional. It's how you start it that matters. Now, do I sometimes hit the snooze too many times and wake up in a panic? Yes. I'm human. But my mornings are set up to be protected from the world so I can focus on where I want to invest my time and attention.

Making intentional changes to your routine, setting boundaries, and keeping track of everything on an attention balance sheet will help you avoid these common attention investing mistakes. By the end of the book, you'll not only have a deep understanding of the influences on your attention but also a tangible example of how your daily attention ledger changes the more aware you are of the social influences at play in your life.

Taking Accountability for Your Investment Mistakes

Right now, you are spending time, attention, and energy reading this book. That is a full investment in this moment. Thank you, by the way. I understand how valuable your attention is and I appreciate yours in this moment. The ROI of this investment is the ability to control and refocus your attention into appreciating life assets that bring an array of ROI that improve your quality of life. When you monitor your attention, time, and energy, you respect them more and spend them well.

With any investment, there needs to be accountability. Blaming the stock market for tanking is naïve. Unless you're investing in treasury bonds or other secured options, the accountability falls on the investor to make wise choices. You can't blame the stock, only the person who invested in it. In your life, that's you. That's *only* you—you're the only one who gives your attention to things. No one can take attention from you for very long. After a certain point, you're approving the transaction and accountable for the outcome.

We've discussed the volatile, risky nature of the social currency market. Volatility means there are certainly opportunities for quick wins, but it's not a wise long-term investment because again, there are no assets being accumulated. All your social investments are liquid. So it's understandable when you're left feeling empty when your main investment has been increasing your social currency over the years.

That's not to say these social currencies hold no value. They certainly do. People have created careers on their social currency, gained incredible wealth, and earned respect. Holding high amounts of social currency has benefits. But like real currency, it's not worth much until you use it for something you need. Social equity is built from investing in people, not currency. No genuine relationships are built on the foundation of beauty, power, or status. That's how the attraction or initial connection begins, but it must go deeper than that.

That's where social currency falls short. When we look to social currency as the foundation for relationships and self-esteem, we quickly see that anyone who values social currency in relationships is only using it to increase their own social portfolio. You aren't building equity with them because they're using the social currency for themselves.

It's transactional.

So, while, yes, you can use this surplus of attention and energy to invest in pursuing social currency to make yourself feel validated in the short term, that will bring you full circle back to this feeling of, "What's next?"

Don't beat yourself up over paying attention to the wrong things. The good part about accountability is that it gives you control over the situation. If your choices caused the problem, your choices can fix the problem.

Speaking of fixing problems, now that you have control over your attention and feel this surplus, what you do next is everything—no pressure, though.

What you give the most daily attention to is what you value most in your life. Remember, you get to choose how your life feels. You can't change the circumstances of your life overnight, but you can change how you feel in those circumstances by directing your attention wisely.

So now it's time to decide where it's going to go. By now, you know where it's been going and you know the mistakes people make when investing attention. Now you get to be strategic about investing.

Start by investing that attention into yourself to rest for a few days (or weeks) first and give yourself a complete reset. Your attention and energy will feel focused and whole. It won't be scattered. You won't be addicted to the validation of social currency, and you can pursue life with a clear head. This is the best place to be before making investment decisions and selecting your life assets.

A meaningful life comes from investing in life assets that align with your values. These are things that appeal to you and reflect your beliefs. Life assets allow you to experience the purpose of life. Am I about to tell you I know the purpose of life? Actually, yes.

The Purpose of Life

The purpose of life is simple. You and I are here to enjoy, express, and connect. I formed this worldview after processing an existential crisis related to my own body, my purpose, and why I felt like nothing I did was "enough."

Focusing on my body was the perfect starting point. If you want to know the purpose of life, the vehicle we're given provides lots of clues. I asked questions about my body's purpose. I approached it objectively, like I would something I didn't have an emotional attachment to. I thought back to my philosophy courses and started a thought exercise.

If aliens landed on Earth and found a chair, what would they look for to know what it is and how to use it? Things that are confusing, or seemingly unnecessary, become the biggest clues to what its purpose might be. The obvious reasons aren't always helpful because it can be too broad to know the true purpose.

A car gets you from A to B, sure, but so do boats, trains, and bicycles. So, you must look at the specifics to see the deeper purpose of a vehicle. The chair exercise is simple, but doing this with the human body took some time.

For example, why do we need sleep? Why do we have taste buds? There are biological functions for these things, of course, but when you boil it down, there are a lot of things that seem "extra." Things like smell, taste, touch, sight, etc. Your senses aren't absolutely essential to staying alive, but they make being alive more enjoyable. We could've been designed like flowers where we get energy through photosynthesis. Sunlight could fuel our lives. But God said, "No, let's give them some variety and enjoyment in how they get energy." We could've been designed like trees where we are stationary, not able to move through the world, but God said, "No, let's give them bodies that move and grow so they can express themselves, connect with others, and explore the world."

Everything our body does can be linked back to one of the life purposes of enjoyment, expression, and connection. Taste buds are for enjoyment. Hair is for warmth and protection, but the fact it looks different on everyone also points to expression. Falling asleep next to someone creates an opportunity for connection.

Voices are for enjoyment, expression, and connection. Movement is for all three purposes, as well. I could keep going, but I won't.

So, when you think about life assets, they are things that produce the purposes of enjoyment, expression, and connection. Life assets fall under the categories of health, creativity, and growth. Each of these create opportunities to enjoy, express, and connect.

Health is physical, mental, relational, emotional, and spiritual. Without your health, good luck enjoying much of anything. When I'm physically sick, I don't get to express myself in fun ways—sometimes, I can barely stay conscious long enough to express anything. Poor health is a hindrance to our purpose. Poor health prevents us from connecting with others, as well. Think about quarantine in 2020.

Creativity lends to an increased ability to enjoy yourself, express yourself, and connect with others. Think about when you have a new idea you're excited about. You call your go-to idea friend and share the news. You connect with them, you enjoy the idea, and by bringing the idea to life, you have expressed part of who you are and what you believe.

Growth allows you to enjoy things you otherwise wouldn't have had the opportunity to experience. When your abilities, intellect, or world view grows, you have opportunities to express yourself in new ways. When I moved to Los Angeles, it was outside my comfort zone. I was exposed to new industries, opportunities, and projects I would never have had access to by staying in the Midwest. I grew because of it, and my enjoyment, expression, and connection expanded.

All these areas are worth pursuing on their own, regardless of the social currency that might accompany them.

The validation that comes with social currency can only mimic these feelings. A mirror does not create a human being when I stand in front of it; it merely reflects what already exists. Mirrors are useful, but no one believes they actually create anything new. In the same way, there's nothing tangible about social currency; the value is found in what it's reflecting. Compliments are great, but they're most impactful when they reflect one of your life assets, not your social currency.

The more life assets you invest in, the more purposeful your life feels. You enjoy yourself more. You have opportunities and space to express yourself regularly. You are more connected with people around you.

Where do you start?

As you can imagine, there are endless life assets that fall under these three categories. This is exciting. You get to experiment to see which resonate with your interests, your talents, and your pace of life.

The best part is, your life assets will change as you grow. Just like with financial investments, when you start out, your options are limited, but as you accumulate wealth and assets, more investment opportunities open up to you.

Remember, you are the only one responsible for how your life feels. You get to choose the life assets you invest in, and you are always allowed to, what? Quit. Change your mind. Give up. Try new things.

For me, I started rock climbing (health), practicing violin (creativity), and writing this book (growth). I embarked on these things only *after* a period of true rest, during which I came to understand the difference between spending time developing life assets versus productivity for productivity's sake. Investing in life assets focuses on patience; investing in productivity focuses on praise. The three new assets I invested in continue to engage my mind, body, and heart, and they continue to give me a return on my attention investment. After just six months of violin lessons, I could play a nice little Bach song. My teacher says I have an incredibly natural bow hold. That feels good. I'm in no rush to get on a stage or have anyone hear this song to feel proud of who I'm becoming. The fact I'm progressing and able to play the instrument feels good.

Action Steps

It's time to take these concepts off the page and start creating real change in your life. Be sure to balance your choices between physical activities, creative pursuits, intellectual growth, and relational expansion. Choose a few and try it out. Make your life feel great to live every day. Make yourself proud of who you're becoming.

PART THREE:

Paying Attention

CHAPTER 16

Fakers Gonna Fake

In 2020, I moved to Los Angeles, CA, home of the Lakers, crowded beaches, insane traffic, and the world's most artificially beautiful people.

The realization that everyone here has work done surprised me more than I'm proud to admit. At first, I didn't notice because I assumed all the beautiful people from small towns across the world moved here to fulfill the classic Hollywood story. Then my roommate turned me on to the telltale signs of a nose job and every kind of filler you can imagine. One you see it, you can't unsee it. And I quickly learned it's not just women who are artificially beautiful in L.A.; it's everyone.

Because of the progress I made in my body image and self-worth, I was sure I wouldn't be impacted by any ideas of editing my face that swirled around conversations, handshakes, and side eyes from strangers. But being surrounded by straight noses makes you question yours, even if you never thought about changing it. But for me, who seriously considered a nose job when I was younger, it stirred up those old thoughts telling me I would be a better version of me if I "fixed" my rounded nose.

I found myself studying the lines in my forehead with a new-found action plan of, *Maybe if I just…* and *What about a little…* Those thoughts crept in, and I caught them quickly. But a different version of myself would have let them settle in. I used to let those thoughts get comfortable and take up space until they became strong enough to move me into action. Even though these particular thoughts were pushed away as quickly as they arrived, I let them linger longer than I expected.

This, coming from me. I have courses teaching women how to feel comfortable in their imperfect bodies. I created a method to build body confidence rooted in the purpose of a body, and even I wasn't fully immune to the pressure to fake it a little. The sheer availability of a quick fix makes the temptation strong. When artificial bodies are normalized, natural bodies are scrutinized. We become vulnerable to falling into what's expected rather than focusing on what's important.

This pressure exists in all forms of social currency. You might be tempted to fake your power and status by renting foreign cars, wearing knock-off designer or diamonds, and making your job title sound more impressive than it actually is. You can easily autotune your voice, buy followers, and pay your child's way into prestigious Ivy League institutions.

But faking your body is the most personal. The effect it has on your perception of yourself is deep. I'm going to focus on this pressure to fake social currency because of the impact it has on relationships, health, and culture, but know that this example is true of what happens when you fake any social currency. It leads to a deep sense of inadequacy.

Let's say you're not tempted to go all in with changing your body. Maybe you're not interested in the permanent (or even semi-permanent) cosmetic procedures. You're safe right? Wrong.

Even if you're not ready to trade real for fake and want to keep your natural face and body as it is, that's not preventing you from falling into a trap of editing. The allure of built-in filters on every social media app and cellphone makes it simple to swap out your bare skin for a sheen of color, plumped lips, and even a slimmer nose, depending on the filter.

The easier it becomes to fake the airbrushed look, the harder it becomes to distinguish between which features are real and which are fake. Even within my own mind. I remember making a conscious decision that everything I posted on IG stories would be my real face without a filter. As the months went by, I found myself hiding from stories when I didn't look good. I would turn my camera on to record and quickly close it out because the lighting was bad. Or I would record and delete videos over and over until I decided it was better to wait until I looked more "polished" to talk about the topic.

None of it penetrated my self-confidence like it used to, but it stopped me from showing up for the women who needed me. For me, that's what it always comes back to: How can I help the person who feels alone right now?

The truth is, I wasn't helping anyone by protecting my own ego and self-image. I felt guilty for prioritizing that over my purpose.

After reflection, consideration, and going back and forth on whether or not I was keeping my word, I changed my mind. I decided using certain filters would be okay. Ones that don't distort anything about my actual face or bone structure but make me look similar to when I wear makeup. That way I didn't have to take the time to do my makeup and still felt polished while sharing stories. For the most part, it's a life saver. My pores have thanked me, but I still wonder now and then if I'm leading a good example or giving in to the pressures to look perfect. The filters I use are noted on the story, so my followers can see I'm using a filter, but that assumes people pay attention to that.

Once I got a message from my cousin about how good my teeth looked, and she asked what I use to get them so white.

Immediately, I felt that familiar sting called shame. The feeling of being found out.

Was it a complete lie? No. I have white teeth. People compliment me on my smile in person, but the filter definitely made them look whiter. I quickly typed out a response, thanking her for noticing, recommending my Crest 3D White toothpaste and calling out the filter that worked faster than sodium fluoride ever could.

It's okay to edit photos. It's okay to use certain filters. The important part is being transparent about what is real and what is edited. This is true for other forms of social currency as well. It's okay to rent cars. It's okay to have fake diamonds, but don't pretend it's something that it's not.

Put Your Real Self Out There

It's getting harder to tell what's real and what's not, and not just when it comes to touched-up selfies. In the age of dating apps, it's increasingly easy to curate a persona that covers up any flaws you feel you have, whether physical or otherwise. Instead of presenting an accurate picture of themselves, so many people share the version they want to be, or neglect to mention certain insecurities they have. Outside the dating app world, this is true of every Instagram profile as well. It's just that instead of trying to impress a potential date, you're trying to impress a potential follower.

This fake dating profile trend never made sense to me, maybe because I'm a Scorpio and we're wired to be honest to a fault. If you use a fake version of yourself to match with someone, how is that going to benefit your relationship success in the long run?

Using outdated or highly edited photos sets everyone up for failure. Posing in front of someone else's Ferrari to get a date is only going to attract someone who is attracted to that Ferrari. But people looking for a real relationship are open to people who aren't the number one choice in the superficial departments, but whose profiles actually show they have similar interests and a personality.

Think about it. I wouldn't want to be in a relationship (romantic or otherwise) with someone who's attracted to an edited version of me. Always needing to live up to a filtered version of my face or half-truths about my career success, education, or financial status? No, thank you. That sounds exhausting. And here's the thing, meaningful relationships are about truth, trust, and growing together. You can't have that when you start with deception. Whether you're dating or not, focus on who you are, expand who you are, and fall in love with who you are becoming. When you do that, you'll attract friends, colleagues, followers, and partners who are invested in you, not your social currency.

> By showcasing your real personality, you'll attract people who like...you!

Who Do You Want to Attract?

There are hundreds of dating apps, a handful of good ones, and as a rule I only have one profile at a time. I cannot keep track, I do not want to keep track, and it takes too much of my energy to manage the one that I often delete it after four or five days.

Hinge is my preferred dating app—don't ask me why. I've gone on over 40 first dates in the three years I've been single. Some dates left me deleting the app and pledging to swear off men for a while. Other dates left me opening the app to see who'd messaged me since I got home. It's such a weird time to be alive.

Even with my notifications-off rule, Hinge gets addictive. Knowing there are always more guys waiting for you at the tap of a finger does something to your brain and makes the app hard to ignore.

The important thing to understand about using these apps (and a lesson that applies to all your digital profiles) is that you really do get what you put out. I think of dating like fishing; you won't catch walleye with worms. There are many variables that go into catching the fish you're after. Time of day, weather, bait, location, etc. Which led me to a few experiments I've done with my profile.

Once, for science, I only used what I would call "sexy" pictures on my profile—pictures of me dressed up, doing nothing.

I answered the prompts in the most basic way I knew how. I tried to make it so there was no personality whatsoever, just the social currency of beauty in the form of sex appeal. Under job title, I put model—which didn't feel like lying because anyone can be a self-proclaimed Instagram model, right?

This profile blew up within minutes. Minutes. There were guys validating "me" left and right. All projecting their dream girl onto this blank canvas of a profile I created. They called me smart, funny, and interesting even though I put no more than 12 words total on this profile. Can you imagine if I met up with any of these guys? I wouldn't know how to act or what to say. I'd constantly feel nervous about them "finding out" I'm not really who I led them to believe I was. And yet, that's how some people approach dating, friendships, and their career. An exhausting attempt at seeing how far they can get trying to be someone impressive, paranoid the whole time they might find out.

Another time, I used photos that showed my achievements. I was shown accepting awards, speaking on stage, and wearing glasses. I answered the prompts to highlight my professional achievements, graduating from college in three years, and paying off all my debt.

This profile also blew up within minutes.

The types of guys each profile attracted were extremely different. This experiment taught me a valuable lesson in dating and life; You will always attract someone, but the question is: Who do you want to attract?

An Influence Worth Having

You see this in the content creator world. If you put out funny content, you will attract followers who want to laugh. If you put out political content, you will attract followers who want to get angry. If you put out controversial content, you will attract followers who want drama.

This is why showing social currency is complicated. When you have a lot of it, it's difficult to hide, and you shouldn't have to be dishonest about who you are. However, you will attract some people who only value the social currency you have and don't care about you as a person. You get attention for the things you have, not the person you are. This gets confusing and frustrating. It's why even beautiful, powerful, influential people can feel lonely, used, and discarded.

Even though you have the attention of millions of people, you don't feel known by any of them. It's difficult to trust who is invested in *you* and who is invested in what you can do for them. It's important to avoid resting on social currency to form friendships or attract partners. The only way to be accepted for who you truly are is to show people who you truly are. You must learn how to be vulnerable and gage the response of people in your life. This is another way the social currency graph from Chapter 5 is helpful.

The people who blindly tolerate your poor behavior are valuing you based on your social currency. The people who set boundaries with you and are willing to walk away are actually invested in a real relationship. It will be challenging, but rewarding to stick with the high-self-worth people who don't tolerate your tantrums.

So the next time you post a picture or create a profile, I want you to try doing it with the purpose of connecting on a meaningful level. Don't just upload the picture you think shows the most social currency. Show what you want people to know about you. Show something that's vulnerable. Show something that's real.

Faking Social Currency

When you're pretending to be more impressive than you actually are, it makes impressive things seem ordinary. It dilutes it. The bar for impressive is raised, artificially, and suddenly no one feels good enough unless they're boosting their social currency in some capacity. In short, faking social currency causes inflation in the market.

It's like in powerlifting when everyone is taking steroids; you have to take them just to keep up. Even if you are the strongest naturally, you'll always lose to someone on steroids. The competitors know that's just part of the game.

This is what's happening with how easy it is to fake social currency. Everyone starts doing it here and there, and soon enough you're building a completely fake persona. Then you feel like you must maintain the persona across all digital platforms and intro real life.

Something interesting happens when we're complimented for something that isn't real. It doesn't fulfill us in the same way because we know we're being validated for a lie. A version of this also happens when we're doing things simply for validation. Even when we get it, it doesn't feel as good as when you do something for the simple fact that you enjoy it or believe in it.

You're getting validated by something you didn't actually like or don't truly enjoy. Validation is important, and you can seek it for healthy reasons. However, when the means by which you're getting validation don't resonate with you, there's an emptiness, a feeling of fraud or deception.

Insecurity Is Loud. Confidence Is Quiet.

Speaking of feeling like a fraud, everyone has insecurities, and the easiest way to spot them is paying attention to what someone brags about. If you feel like you need to flex, it's because you want to prove you're strong. You want someone to validate you. This insecurity triggers desperation, and understandably so. When you value social currency and don't have it, you don't want anyone to find out, so you fake it. When you value social currency and have it, you control the conversation to focus on what you have.

Confident people don't talk much about themselves. They have nothing to prove; they're not competing. They don't need the attention, validation, or approval from others—they're looking for connection. They don't feel like something is lacking within them. They simply are who they are, without shoving it in anyone's face, and they don't worry about rejection.

I hear you thinking, *But I don't want to be rejected. That's why I hide behind my social currency. That's why I always go back to, "But I'm rich, but I'm attractive, but I have an Oscar...they would be stupid not to like me!"* because with that thinking, they actually aren't rejecting you. The things you listed aren't who you are, they are money, looks, and a trophy. It feels safer to transact in social currency than be vulnerable enough to open up. The danger with doing this is that you will never be fully known, plus your attention is still on social currency.

You will soon prioritize social currency in others. Eventually, you stop seeing people for their humanity, and only see them for their social currency. They become a commodity. The very thing you lamented about other people doing to you will become true of your treatment of them.

Not only does it begin with objectifying and commoditizing others, but it also grows into objectifying and commoditizing the relationship you have with yourself.

Self-objectification is the ultimate insecurity because we no longer see our intrinsic worth, only what we have to offer other people. We become used to judging other people that way, we judge ourselves by the same metrics and no longer see worth in who we are unless we are performing, being validated, and winning the social currency game. This is what leads us to measure our worth based on number of IG followers, YouTube subscribers, job offers, lovers, etc. It's a dangerous road to go down because the farther you go on it, the harder it becomes to tell whether followers, friends, and even family members love you for *you* or just for your social currency. This leads to more insecurity because we fear that the moment someone comes along with more social currency (a more expensive car, a hotter body, more trophies), the people in our lives will leave us.

TAKEAWAY

Doubting if the people you care about most truly care about you is the loneliest feeling in the world. I like being alone sometimes, but I hate feeling lonely. Using social currency, when you have it, is the easiest way to feel accepted. It's also the easiest way to feel used.

Which brings us back to the central point of this chapter: Fakers gonna fake, but you don't have to be one of them. You won't know for sure if someone loves you or your social currency unless you show them who you really are. This requires vulnerability. Leading with who you *are* instead of your social currency means the thing open for rejection is you. It also means the thing open for acceptance is you. And when you have those people in your life, you never need to fake it.

CHAPTER 17

Moving Beyond Your Inherited Social Currency

It's pretty obvious there are vast inequalities in the distribution of social currency. And while it's true that social currency can be accumulated by anyone who is willing to put in enough effort, a big factor in the balance of your social currency "account" is what you're born into.

Imagine a beautiful baby girl born to a Harvard-educated CEO mother and an A-list celebrity father. Within weeks of her birth, her picture-perfect cherub face will appear in magazines and every Instagram timeline (thanks to Dad), and by the time she's old enough to apply to colleges, she'll have every advantage imaginable at Ivy League institutions (thanks to Mom). If she's lucky enough to have inherited her parents' talents (intelligence from her mother, acting ability from her father) or if she has a talent of her own (let's say musical or artistic ability), there is virtually no door that will be closed to her. This is the reality of inherited social currency.

Of course, most of us aren't born with quite this much social currency to start with. You might be "small-town famous" (e.g., the child of a former homecoming queen and the town high school's star quarterback) but once you venture beyond that small town, you'll find your inherited social currency isn't worth much of anything.

While this feels just as unfair as the inequalities in actual currency and wealth, remember that not everyone values social currencies the same. What's desirable to you might not be desirable to me. Instead of focusing on the unequal distribution of currency, which you can't control, your attention is better spent in understanding what social currency you currently value, whether you want to continue valuing that, and then investing your energy accordingly.

No matter what social currency you inherit, it causes fear and anxiety when you put too much value on it. When you have high amounts of social currency, you feel guilty for having more than others and fearful you will lose it. It becomes a prison you feel you must maintain in order to preserve the love and acceptance in your life. When you have low amounts of social currency, you feel shame for having less than others and fear you will never gain the level of influence you desire.

Abundance and Guilt

My dad's business started doing well when I was in third grade. Before that, my family of seven people and one dog lived in a three-bedroom rambler. We mostly ate oatmeal, mac and cheese with hot dogs, and buttered rice. Growing up I didn't realize how poor we were. Kudos to my mother for making it feel like going clothes shopping at the Salvation Army was normal. We honestly had no idea. By the time I was in high school, things changed. We wore the brands all the cool kids had and even set some of the trends. White belts, ripped jeans from Hollister, and puffer vests with fur-lined hoods. It was the early 2000s; the rise of our jeans had never been lower.

My mom got her Chrysler upgraded to a Lexus when my sister turned 17. Even though he could afford it, Stephen Buege wasn't one to show off his money or spoil his children by getting us our own car, so he timed this purchase with the need for another "kid car."

Even the most responsible decisions turn into gossip when there's literally nothing else to do. Rumors spread in a town that size, and soon the story sounded quite different.

"She got a brand new car for her birthday."
"The Buege girls are spoiled because their dad owns his own business."
"I heard they get all their clothes from the Mall of America."

The funny part is, these rumors weren't even interesting. Obviously, they weren't true, but they also weren't juicy or dramatic. Even if my sister did get a brand-new car for her birthday, it's not like she got the Lexus. It was a Chrysler—big deal. Yeah, my dad was a partner in a business, but it's not like my dad was Glenn Taylor (the billionaire founder of Taylor Corporation, owner of the Minnesota Timberwolves, and resident of Mankato, MN, of all places).

And let's say, for argument sake, we did get our clothes at the Mall of America. Anyone who's been there knows how overrated it is. Nothing to brag about. So for *that* to be the rumor tells you exactly what you need to know about the people spreading them.

But this illustrates the assumptions made about people born into social currency. Our family gained the status of "wealthy" because we had a custom-built home, my dad owned a business, and we wore trendy clothes. But it was like, small-town Minnesota trendy. Let's not get ahead of ourselves. Without the proper context, people made assumptions that we always had money and we were shallow and stuck up because of the kind of house we lived in and the clothes we wore.

They assumed my siblings and I were spoiled—even though I've paid my own cell phone bill since I got my LG flip phone on my 14th birthday. We were comfortable, but far from spoiled.

I found myself with a certain level of resentment towards the assumptions people made about social currency I didn't ask for. It's one thing to work hard to become a fitness model, study relentlessly to pursue an Ivy League business education, or build your success and wealth from the ground up. People can judge you all they want for that. You pursued that social currency and can defend those judgments because you earned it. But what about the judgments from people about things you didn't choose? Things you didn't earn but were handed down to you by your family?

When you inherit social currency, there's a burden of expectation. Being born into a family of doctors creates the expectation you, too, should become one. Being born beautiful creates an environment where people expect things to be true about you without getting to know your mind or your heart. They just look at your body and reach a conclusion. Social currency doesn't always carry the advantage people imagine.

People will resent the person who owns the thing they covet. If you have good looks, they'll assume you're only successful because you've been favored due to your physical appearance. It's a double-edged sword because you're expected to be attractive, but if you're *too* attractive, people will start rumors about you or assume you never earned anything because you must have skated by on your looks.

It has nothing to do with you and everything to do with the posture of their heart. Don't let anyone convince you that your blessings are taking away from theirs.

While it's not your fault you have this social currency, it is a responsibility that you must learn to manage. Much is expected from those to whom much is given.

You have an opportunity many people aren't afforded. You are entrusted with this attention. You are called to steward it with wisdom. None of that is easy. Many people crumble under the pressure, unable to live up to those expectations. It's difficult to know how to steward something you didn't earn because you don't understand it as well as the person who earned it. Some who inherit social currency resist it entirely and abandon the gifts at their disposal because the guilt of not feeling they deserve them is crushing.

Whether you deserve them or not, these are the circumstances of your life. You get to decide how you respond to them. You can either shrink back from the responsibility and question if you're deserving, or you can *become* deserving by rising to the calling to steward your influence.

Enjoy and use the social currency you inherit, but don't let it become the master of your attention. Don't let the availability of social currency define who you are or allow the pressure to shape a path that isn't meant for you.

Scarcity and Shame

On the flip side, if you didn't inherit a lot of (or any) social currency, you've probably noticed that an empty social wallet makes you feel embarrassed or defensive.

Think of the first time you were bullied. What was it for? I bet it was because you lacked some form of social currency. Maybe you didn't wear the right shoes in middle school, your teeth were crooked, or you bombed your audition for the solo in choir.

Shame is used to humiliate us into changing our behavior. It's a form of negative behavioral adjustment rooted in feelings of inadequacy and unhappiness. Therefore, the first step toward conquering it is recognizing that happiness has very little to do with the amount of social currency you have and everything to do with your life assets.

The beauty of life assets is that we all start from zero. Remember that lucky little girl I painted a picture of earlier in the chapter? The one with every opportunity at her feet, and doors open all around her? She may have inherited a massive amount social currency, but when it comes to her life assets—her mind, body, and heart—she's born with a blank slate just like the rest of us.

So if you find yourself in a position of scarcity, feeling inadequate compared to those around you who inherited more social currency, remember that you have just as much power as they do to invest your attention into your life assets, which you know are more important. There are no excuses when it comes to building these assets, so don't let your lack of inherited social currency be a crutch.

Action Steps

Awareness is always the first step to solving any addiction, problem, or pattern—not to mention overcoming feelings of guilt, shame, or inadequacy. To become aware of what is holding you back, you first need to identify what social currency you were born with and how you were taught to value it.

To Identify the forms of social currency you resent versus the types you desire, try tracing the forms of social currency you were taught to value growing up. If you came from a wealthy family, that could create strong positive or negative associations with money, power, etc. If your parents talked a lot about the way people look, you could have been conditioned to value beauty.

Ask a friend to do the same and compare how you value different social currencies. The differences will show you in a close-to-home, real-life example how differently people value things. Seeing this firsthand will help you challenge some of the things you feel pressure to value and unlock the potential to actually pursue things YOU care about, instead of what your parents taught you to value.

CHAPTER 18

Enjoying Your Social Currency Without Greed

As I'm writing this, I'm sitting at my favorite cafe in Larchmont, a neighborhood in L.A. I came here on a whim to do some writing. I ordered a fresh pressed beet juice with ginger, lemon, and all the other L.A. essentials you can practically order on IV drip. It cost $16. I didn't care. I wanted it.

The Midwestern penny pincher in me screamed, "For juice?!" And the California free spirit in me responded, "Yeah, let's see what it's like!"

Because I know I'm not exactly strapped for cash anymore. I have a handle on my finances, investments, and business. I worked through the weird relationship I had with money from growing up poor. I now see money for what it is, an amazing tool for making life fun. I can use it to bring me closer to others, enjoy myself, and express myself. Money is a tool to make life easier; it's not life itself.

The brightly pigmented purple caught my attention before the server could say, "You are gifted," while setting it down. I was brimming with excitement. It tasted better than it looked; worth the money times two, plus 20 percent gratuity. What a fun experience to enjoy.

That's my new relationship with money. Money didn't change, but how I use it, think about it, and feel about it is different. That's my new relationship with social currency as well. I don't care what social currency it costs; I want the things that will bring me health, peace, and community. I pay full attention to people I'm intrigued by, regardless of what they can "do for me." Regardless of whether it seems "expensive" at first, it's about the experience more than anything else.

Very few things are inherently good or bad; what makes them one or the other is the context in which we use them. Social currency is a tool, just like financial currency. When you love it too much, there's greed. You sacrifice what truly matters in exchange for a little more. What you have never feels like enough.

Greed with social currency turns people into commodities. You use people for what they can get for you and leave them when they've served their purpose. This desensitizes you to feelings of empathy and compassion.

You see this in L.A. everywhere. The city is a living case study of social currency in action. An older man entices a young woman to sleep with him by buying her expensive gifts, taking her on trips, and offering to bank rolling her BBL and boob job. After she levels up her status and beauty, she leaves him for a man who offers something different. A man rents a house in the Hollywood hills for a few months and throws a party every weekend. He tells guests he just bought the home and pitches them on investing in his new "flourishing" business. These are each real stories I've seen happen. Everyone is trying to level up their beauty, power, and status, but what they don't realize is there's never an end to this vicious cycle when it's driven by the insatiable greed for social currency.

But when you release your attachment to social currency—when you respect it and understand the power it has—you can use it freely for good purposes and enjoy it. Once you earn your social currency passively through life assets, your attention will be in a much healthier place. You won't feel a sense of lack. You'll be investing in things that matter to you.

When you get social currency without trying—which comes from your life assets, by the way—it's easy to spend it and not think twice. You have a good relationship with it because you're not addicted to it, and you know it will replenish.

> You can have a problem with greed whether you are broke or a billionaire, and the same is true for social currency. You don't need a lot of it to get possessive and inadvertently hurt people. The best way to use social currency to your advantage without abusing anyone is to purposefully invest attention into people and causes you believe in, not things you think will get the most attention.

Social Altruism: Lending Your Social Currency to a Good Cause

When you find yourself in the fortunate position of having accumulated a large amount of social currency (whether you inherited it or busted your butt to earn every penny), you'll have some choices to make about how to spend it. You have a platform—and the attention of thousands or even millions of people—so what are you going to direct their attention to? Will you bask in their attention and turn it back on yourself? If you're an actor, are you going to continue to just put out movies? If you're wealthy, are you only going to continue filling your bank account? Or are you going to lend your social currency to a cause you believe in, drawing the attention you're getting towards something people can do to fix problems in the world?

Personally, I believe that when you have people paying attention to you, you have a certain responsibility to speak up about the things that people need to be talking about. We've all heard the cliché, "With great power comes great responsibility." It's the same with great beauty, great talent, great social status, and so on. Remember how I said earlier that social currency is a tool that can be used for better or worse? Social altruism is possibly the best use of the tool there is.

What does social altruism look like?

Fortunately, our pop culture is full of great examples of celebrities lending their social currency to important issues. There are plenty to choose from, but I'll focus on a few of my personal favorites.

Remember Ashton Kutcher, pretty boy of the early 2000s? He could've just basked in the glow of his fame and celebrity for decades, making movies and taking on projects that reinforce his heartthrob status. Instead, he started a nonprofit, THORN, that aims to put a stop to child sex trafficking. People are quick to criticize actors for making public statements or dipping their toes into global/political issues, making comments along the lines of, "You're an actor. Stick to your day job." But in Ashton Kutcher's case, he made it his day job to do something about an issue he cares about deeply, and he uses his considerable social currency to amplify that message. In other words, he used his influence for good.

And, of course, you remember Colin Kaepernick of the San Francisco 49ers famously taking a knee during the National Anthem to protest against police brutality and systemic racism in America. This simple act could have been performed by any-one (and has been, many times before), but it took someone of Kapernick's fame and status for the message to be amplified loud enough for the whole country to have a conversation about it. Now Kaepernick considers himself a civil rights activist first, and former football player second.

I can hear you saying, "Alright, Rebekah, that's fine, but what about people who aren't rich and famous? Is social altruism exclusive for those who have high amounts of social currency to throw at a cause?"

Fortunately, you don't have to be a celebrity to use your social currency in an altruistic way. You can take whatever social cur-rency you've accumulated—no matter how modest the amount—and influence the attention of your circle of friends, fans, and followers. You can share a deserving GoFundMe post to widen its reach. You can let everyone know about a nonprofit you donated to and encourage them to do the same (although be careful to do this for the right reasons, and not just to increase your own social currency—virtue signaling can be a cry for attention). Something as simple as being excited about a project you're working on or supporting can inspire people to find something they're excited to support, even if it's not the same thing.

Social altruism doesn't just occur on social media, remember? You can use your social currency to help other people get ahead, such as recommending a qualified but lesser-known candidate to your boss who's looking to make a new hire. Social currency can also help you advocate for people who need it. If they're under fire, you can vouch for them, and your word —as a person with high social currency will influence other people's perceptions.

One note of caution: there's a balance you need to strike in order for people to take your social altruism seriously. I see stories about influencers who accumulate millions of fans and followers and attempt unsuccessfully to pivot the attention of those followers to something else. You see it with a lot of Instagram models. When they try to lend their social currency to an issue they care about, they'll find that no one wants to hear their thoughts on the subject. When they try to start a brand or business, they complain, "No one is taking me seriously as an entrepreneur." Well, I'm not surprised. If you got millions of followers by posting hundreds of photos of your booty in a bikini—essentially making your profile into a free Playboy magazine—those same people are not necessarily going to listen to your heartfelt message about Alzheimer's research or buy your line of activewear. Just because you have someone's attention doesn't mean they're going to take your advice.

So if you find yourself in this position, take a step back. You need to grow your influence in a way that's going to set you up to be credible when you want to speak up on something other than the thing you're most known for. Gwyneth Paltrow is a great example of someone who managed to do this successfully. Despite coming up as an actress, she was also interested in health and wellness as well as doing humanitarian work. She branched out early in her career and slowly but surely became known for all three things. Now she owns the lifestyle brand Goop and participates in many charity fundraisers. It was a seamless expansion because she took her time, built up credibility in new areas, and eventually created a highly successful empire.

TAKEAWAY

You can be cheap or generous with whatever amount of social currency you have. The more social currency you have, the more opportunities you have to invest it in a good cause. If you're looking to pivot into social altruism, start with something naturally aligned with the reason you have the influence you do. This can take time to expand into, but it's worth it to create a rewarding life asset.

CHAPTER 19

Unexpected ROIs

When I moved to California, I helped a friend repot succulents on his rooftop. I've always enjoyed gardening and I like plants, but back in Minnesota I couldn't keep plants alive long enough to enjoy them. Buying more felt mean. I knew bringing them home was a death sentence.

But seeing these plants grow like crazy gave me hope that maybe even I couldn't stand in the way of California sunshine working its magic. I asked if I could take a few pieces with me and give it a try. I had a small pot from an orchid I killed a few months before taunting me in my kitchen.

He gave me some pieces to propagate and try to keep alive (or as he called it, "grow"). He told me to take pictures and document the progress. I rolled my eyes and reluctantly followed directions. My failure isn't exactly something I want proof of. One morning, I looked at my not-growing plants, about to throw them away. Another failed experiment, further confirming my inability to keep plants alive, even if they're "impossible to kill."

But before I tore them out of my little pot, I looked at the picture from 13 days earlier. Expecting no changes, I was shocked to see that several of them looked different. One, in particular, used to be a thin brown stick and now had several green buds growing out of it. I took the clear pot out from the inside and gasped when I saw the root system underneath. In just a few short weeks, the pieces filled the small container with roots.

Two lessons apply here:

First, most of the growth happens underneath the surface. When you start removing social currency from your daily (or, let's be honest, hourly) routine, it's not going to give immediate rewards. Most of the growth is happening underneath the surface. You won't see a difference on the surface for a while.

Second, the only way to measure growth is to actually measure it. Not to think about it or guess, but actually measure. The picture gave proof that my plants had, in fact, grown. They grew more than I expected, and I went from feeling frustrated with myself to feeling embarrassingly proud of this little plant.

So what you're going to do is write down what your life assets currently look like. Then, schedule three weeks from now in your calendar. Create an event to check in on how your life assets are growing. When I feel frustrated with my violin progress, I watch a video of me first starting out, barely able to play Twinkle, Twinkle, and I'm quickly reminded my work is paying off. Remember, you can make adjustments to your goals or even quit if you decide you don't like it. You're allowed to try something and give up.

The goal is simply to try new things. Don't be confined by expectations or pressure from culture, your parents, or even yourself (because those internal thoughts and pressures came from somewhere else to begin with, anyway).

Patience is everything. All good investments take time to pay off. If you look at your Robinhood account on any given day, you're likely to see an increase or decrease of a few dollars in your account and wonder, *What am I even doing this for?* It's not until you look back over a whole year (or five or ten) that you'll be able to see if your strategy is paying off.

Notice I said "if" your strategy is paying off. Not all investments pay off, you must be prepared for that, but that doesn't mean there was no value in making the investment. This is true for relational and financial investments.

If I invest in a tech startup, the owner of the company is going to benefit whether or not I see a dime. Other people benefit, too, like the employees and their families. The field itself may even make progress thanks to my contribution. So even if something goes wrong, and I don't get a return on my investment, I know it wasn't worthless in the grand scheme of life, because other people benefited. While I had a financial loss, there was a gain experienced by others.

You might not get a spouse out of the date you've got planned for tonight. You might not book the role you're auditioning for. But that doesn't mean these experiences won't be worthwhile. Someone always stands to gain from an investment, whether it's financial or relational. You must realize the impact your investments truly make. This helps keep you inspired to invest richly in others. Maybe this first date is going to give the person you're meeting hope that good people are still out there. Maybe you'll make the stressed-out casting director's decision easier. The benefits aren't always for you; someone else might benefit. And that's worth something. I may feel a loss of attention, energy, etc., temporarily, but there was a gain experienced by others. Remember, people are not social currency banks. Expecting to get something for yourself leads to constant disappointment. Imagine the ripple effect you can have in the lives of others when you're not depending on the outcome of your social investments to bring you security.

The REAL Measure of Social Net Worth

If having 10 million followers on Instagram doesn't make me feel socially validated, what will? Simple. It's in the richness, dependability, and joy you get and give inside your relationships. That's the measure of your social net worth. You can have social currency for days, but it's quickly taken away from you when the attention shifts or you enter a new social circle.

Once you have the ability to invest your full, undivided attention into your relationships and life assets, you'll find they produce dividends more quickly, or at the very least, you see which investments are worth pursuing long term and which are not.

Establishing an inner circle is the core of your social net worth. These are your "pillar people" who you trust with the deepest, truest parts of yourself—and they trust you with theirs. They could be friends or family. Months or years can go by without staying in constant contact, but these people pick back up like nothing has changed. Because those deep, true parts of you haven't changed, and you both know that.

After this is secure, your investments can include your colleagues, business partners, clients, down to the guy at the coffee shop who remembers your order. Giving your full attention to a stranger during a small encounter can have a surprising level of impact.

How do you interact and transact on a fulfillment level with the people in your life? How present are you emotionally? And for how wide of a circle? Regardless of social currency or social net worth, your value as a human does not change. The value of your relationships will increase drastically, however, when you apply this approach.

TAKEAWAY

If you take one lesson away from this book, let it be that your relational worth cannot be counted by how many people "like" or follow you, but by who will show up when you need them. It's how deeply the people in your life know you and care for you and how deeply you know and care for them. Investing in people—without the expectation to benefit from their social currency—will pay dividends over the long run, leading to true and lasting social wealth.

Paying attention to what everyone is paying attention to tells you a lot about culture. What it doesn't tell you is what's going to be fulfilling to you, for your life. That's something each of us discover and create for ourselves. This changes through our lives. The less enticed we are by social currency, the more freedom we have to continue this exploration and build a meaningful life that feels good; no matter how many people "like" it.

Is your attention consumed by the social currency of beauty?

16 DAYS TO A BETTER BODY IMAGE

Get proven strategies to beat negative self-talk and shift your body image into neutral by visiting *www.thebodyimagesolution.com*

JOIN THE PROGRAM

Revive your relationship with your body by visiting *www.thebodyimagesolution.com*

SUBSCRIBE TO THE PODCAST

What listeners are saying about *Confidently She,*

"She has so much wisdom and such a beautiful way of relaying information."

"She is a light to all of us,"

"If you need a change in your mindset that you have never been able to find, just listen."

"Life changing!"

Acknowledgements

I remember sitting on my bed after a long day in junior high school. An author presented their novel writing process at an assembly. That was the day I promised myself I would write a book. I wanted to see my name at the bottom of a cover and know that it's mine. This dream was consistently met with, "there's no money in books," as if profit was the only measure of worth. That almost crushed my hope of living out this desire that was just beginning to grow in my young heart.

You can't control the attention living out your desires may receive, but you can control if they get done. Speaking of getting it done, I couldn't have completed this project on my own. Or at least, if I had done it myself, you would be reading a much worse version of this book.

Thank you to everyone who pre-ordered this book, who believed in me as an author before anyone else did. Thank you to James West, who raised his hand to help bring structure and order to this massive idea. Thank you to Lexy Hammonds, who didn't let me settle for "good enough," when I was tired of endless revisions. Big thank you to Sara Kocek, my editor, who shaped a good manuscript into a masterpiece.

I hope I made it clear on the pages of this book that it's naive to believe money, recognition, or influence is what makes a project worth doing. Create things you are proud to call your own. Don't measure their worth based on the attention you get. If you need encouragement, tell me about what you're working on - I can't wait to tell you why it's worth it. Email rebekah@rebekahbuege.com

About the Author

Rebekah Buege (pronounced biggie) grew up in a small town in Southern Minnesota. Her introduction to social issues started when she gained national recognition on the collegiate speech & debate team. She spent four years researching, writing, and performing speeches covering topics of social justice, feminism, and equality before graduating with a B.A. in Economics, Political Science, and  Philosophy from Minnesota State University at 21 years old.

After seeing many women close to her suffer in toxic relationships, and experiencing it firsthand, she focused her talents on studying courage, confidence, and self-worth to help reduce the number of vulnerable women at risk for neglect and abuse. In 2017, she created *Confidently She*, a top-rated podcast on iTunes & Spotify, to reach women searching for support.

While living in Los Angeles, California, during 2020, she was invited to judge the Miss California United States pageant. The contestant who won Miss California, Tiffany Rea, credited *Confidently She* as the secret behind her body confidence during the pageant. Tiffany went on to win the Miss United States pageant later that year.

Rebekah launched her signature online program at www.thebodyimagesolution.com and released her first book, *The Body Image Solution*, in 2022. Today, Rebekah offers online programs, confidence coaching, and remains a top performer in her sales career. Rebekah currently lives in Tampa, FL.

A free ebook edition is available with the purchase of this book.

To claim your free ebook edition:

1. Visit MorganJamesBOGO.com
2. Sign your name CLEARLY in the space
3. Complete the form and submit a photo of the entire copyright page
4. You or your friend can download the ebook to your preferred device

A **FREE** ebook edition is available for you or a friend with the purchase of this print book.

CLEARLY SIGN YOUR NAME ABOVE

Instructions to claim your free ebook edition:
1. Visit MorganJamesBOGO.com
2. Sign your name CLEARLY in the space above
3. Complete the form and submit a photo of this entire page
4. You or your friend can download the ebook to your preferred device

Print & Digital Together Forever.

Snap a photo

Free ebook

Read anywhere

CPSIA information can be obtained
at www.ICGtesting.com
Printed in the USA
JSHW021926300623
44068JS00002B/30